MW01681530

YOGIRAJ
SHRI SHRI LAHIRI MAHASHAY

(September 30, 1828 - September 26, 1895)

SHRI SHRI LAHIRI MAHASHAY

Shri Shri Gurabe Namah

Yogiraj
Shri Shri Lahiri Mahashay

By

Prof. Jogesh Chandra Bhattacharya

M.A., P.R.S.

AMRITA FOUNDATION, INC.
Dallas, Texas
1997

Originally
Published in India with the First Edition in 1964
and the Second Edition in 1969,
by Jogesh Chandra Bhattacharya, M.A., P.R.S.
at 'Shrigurudham' in Howrah.

ISBN: 0-937134-20-1

Printed in the United States of America

Amrita Foundation, Inc. is dedicated to the original
Kriyayoga teachings of Shri Shri Lahiri Mahashay
as given to him by Mahavatar Babaji,
and the original, unchanged writings of Paramhansa
(Swami) Yogananda Giri and Swami Dhirananda Giri
(Dr. Basu Kumar Bagchi)
to promote individual communion with God.
This First American Edition
is a reprint of the Second Edition published
in India in 1969, with minor grammatical corrections.
The Publisher's Note and footnotes have been inserted.

The Cover and inside picture of
Shri Shri Lahiri Mahashay is from the personal
collection of Swami Dhirananda Giri
(Dr. Basu Kumar Bagchi).

Published by

Amrita® FOUNDATION, INC.

P.O. Box 190978
Dallas, Texas 75219-0978

श्रीश्रीगुरवे नमः ॥

मङ्गलाचरणम् ।

ॐ दृष्ट्वा भूलोकदुःखं विगलितहृदयः योऽवतीर्णः पृथिव्यां
यो लीलाविग्रहेण प्रकटितमकरोत् श्रीगुरोः सुष्ठुसेवाम् ।
गुह्यं योगस्य वृत्तं वितरति भुवने यः कृपासागरस्तं
वन्दे श्रीअनिलानन्दं रसघनमधुरं श्रीगुरुं विश्वरूपम् ॥

नत्वा गजाननं देवं सर्वसिद्धिप्रदायकम् ।
वाणीं प्रणम्य विरचेद् योगिराजकथामृतम् ॥

श्रीश्रीश्यामाचरणचरणे सहस्रकमले दले ।
मनो मे रमतां नित्यं सच्चिदानन्दसागरे ॥

ॐ मूकं करोति वाचालं पङ्गुं लङ्घयते गिरिम् ।
यत्कृपा तमहं वन्दे श्रीगुरुं शिवविग्रहम् ॥

DEDICATION

To

My Master

Yogiguru Bhagavan

Shrimat Brahmachari Anilanandaji Maharaj.

Master Mine!

It is not for me to probe the depth of the Infinite Bliss that is Shri Shri Lahiri Mahashay. Yet, you bid me write, and I must obey.

Let Thy words be uttered through this frail mortal frame. Let the dust of Thy Lotus Feet be my Guide.

Amen!

PUBLISHER'S NOTE

The publication of this First American Edition of *Yogiraj Shri Shri Lahiri Mahashay* by Amrita Foundation, Inc. was made possible some 20 years ago by one of Paramhansa Yoganandaji's closest and most devoted disciples and rare-chosen lay ministers, Mary Buchanan Silva, wife of the late Edward Silva, and lovingly known as "Kamala" – the name bestowed on her by her Guru Yoganandaji when they met in 1925. Coming to San Francisco in the Fall of 1949 to start and lead the Bay Area Meditation Group, it was through this couple's many, many years of faithful and tireless spiritual service to the Kriyayoga teachings that Kamala and Edward Silva became known as the "Founding Lay Disciples" for the establishment of Yoganandaji's Richmond Temple in Richmond, California in 1971.

True to her nature of serving spiritually, Kamala was always ready to spread the Guru's and Para ParamGuru's writings, and stories of Their illumined lives in the world, especially, to the householder disciples, who more often than not, did not have the opportunity to come in contact with these wondrous accounts collected in the ashrams.

It was just such an occasion that this little book about the saintly and remarkable life of Lahiri Mahashay, direct disciple of Mahavatar Babaji and Father of Kriyayoga, came into the hands of Kamala from friends who had traveled to the ashrams in India. As always, she was eager to share the priceless treasure of Lahiri Baba's life with others. Without hesitation she so reverently passed the book on to Amrita, hoping that some day it would be published for the American devotees of our Kriya Lineage.

Little did we know then that it would be published on the heels of the 1995 celebration of the 100th Anniversary of the Mahasamadhi of Lahiri Mahashay in this country as Shibendu Lahiri, the great grandson of the Yogiraj, took up, as fourth generation householder of the father-to-son dynastic legacy, the Great Kriya Message of Liberation to carry to Truth-seekers everywhere.

With our most humble pronams and deepest devotion Amrita now publishes this edition on the life of Lahiri Mahashay, and welcomes with open heart of profound love His Radiant Son, Shibendu Lahiri.

The Editor

June 15, 1997
Dallas, Texas

Shri Shri Gurabe Namah

PREFACE TO THE FIRST EDITION

The need for a complete biography in English of Yogiraj Shri Shri Shyama Charan Lahiri Mahashay has been very strongly felt. There are chapters on Shri Shri Lahiri Mahashay in the English *Autobiography of a Yogi* by Paramhansa Yogananda, his spiritual grandson. But all the other biographies of this Great Saint are written in Bengali or Hindi.

The present volume is an outcome of a Gracious Command of my beloved Gurudeva Yogiguru Shrimat Brahmachari Anilanandaji Maharaj. How else could I dare to go into the mystery of an astounding spiritual personality like Shri Shri Lahiri Mahashay?

The main outlines of the life of the Yogiraj are the same in all the available versions of his biography. There are, however, a few minor differences in details. In such cases I have followed the descriptions of his great spiritual descendants whose insight can be absolutely relied upon.

Let the fruit of this labor be offered to the Lotus Feet of Shriguru. "Hari Om".

PREFACE TO THE SECOND EDITION

It is a testimony to the Divine Grace of Shri Shri Lahiri Mahashay that the first edition of this book has been well received by devotees all over the world. The second edition is almost a reproduction of the former edition with very slight changes or additions here and there.

The entire effort has been due to the Grace of my Master at whose Lotus Feet I dedicate the present edition of the book as well.

Shri Shri Gurabe Namah

CONTENTS

Shri Shri Gurabe Namah

CHAPTER I

Introduction

A householder was seated in his own drawing room at Benares, in the lotus posture, surrounded by his disciples. His complexion was fair and his body well-built. His dreamy eyes were half-closed, fixed as they were on something not of this earth. The aura of his tranquility pervaded the atmosphere. He was explaining the *Bhagavadgita*. Of a sudden he opened his eyes wide and cried, "I am getting drowned in the sea near Japan, mingled with the consciousness of hundreds of people." And, the next morning, the disciples were surprised to come across the news of a soul-stirring tragic shipwreck in the Japan Sea.

The householder was the greatest Yogi of the 19th Century, whose cosmic consciousness was entirely free from the limitations of space and time. He was Yogiraj Shri Shri Shyama Charan Lahiri Mahashay.

Indeed, the role silently played by Shri Shri Lahiri Mahashay in changing the world-consciousness into a unity through the path of Yoga can never be exaggerated.

'Yoga' in the widest sense of the term includes all Sadhana. As, Yajnavalkya, the great Yogi of ancient India has said:

"संयोगो योग इत्युक्तो जीवात्मपरमात्मनोः" i.e., Yoga is the union of the individual soul with the Paramatman or Infinite Consciousness. The goal of all spiritual practices is the attainment of the same Infinite or Supra Consciousness, by whichever name one may describe it. In this wider sense all spiritual masters are Yogis. There is, however, a particular variety of Sadhana which is called Yoga in a narrower sense. And it is usually in this sense that the word Yoga is used. This Sadhana consists mainly in controlling the Prana-Vayu (breath) with Pranayama and other processes. The Yogi starts with the postulate that the microcosm contains all that is there in the macrocosm. There is a Bengali proverb which states that what is absent in our body is also non-existent in the Universe. The Yogi therefore considers his own body as the temple for worshipping the Paramatma (the Supreme Self). The limited consciousness of a man gradually expands into the vaster world of Cosmic Consciousness till the Sadhaka (devotee) attains complete Self-Realization.[1]

The greatest contribution of Shri Shri Lahiri Mahashay to the world is that he, according to the instructions of his Great Guru Shri Shri Babaji Maharaj, simplified the infinite multiplicity of the processes of Rajayoga into a few stages and made it available to the common man, especially the householder who is simply lost in the wilderness of worldly duties. It is next to impossible for a householder to follow the strict principles of restraint enunciated in the 'Astanga Yoga' of Patanjali. The processes in the Kriyayoga taught by Lahiri Mahashay make us gradually fit to unfold the Divine within ourselves, with much less effort than is usually necessary. Individual Yogis have always been there in India, but due to a great general deterioration in the mass consciousness (owing to the rules of Nature which will be explained in the Appendix), Yogic processes remained circumscribed in the hands of Yogis alone. It was much too difficult for the common man to follow. Only those who would be ready to dedicate their lives to the cause of the Divine, would be initiated into the teachings. Naturally, their number was very small. The greatest section of the people had no opportunity to follow the principles of Yoga even if they might have eagerness for these. It was Yogiraj Shri Shri Shyama Charan Lahiri Mahashay who felt for us at the heart of his heart and spread the Divine Kriyayoga at a time when the world was just getting ripe for a new era of spiritual synthesis.

Besides, from another point of view, the advent of Shri Shri Lahiri Mahashay has a great significance. Through many bloody and terrible wars, the world now-a-days is slowly reaching towards the ideal of international amity and brotherhood. This ideal must be

1. The human body has 3 great nerve-cords. On both sides of the spinal cord there are gangliated cords of sympathetic nerves. Ordinarily the Prana-Vayu moves through the passages within the gangliated cords: Ira and Pingala. But it must move through Susumna (the very subtle passage through the spinal cord) before any success in Sadhana is to be attained. The unfolding of this passage is called the rousing of the Kundalini or the spiritual force latent in every man.

realized, if the human race is to persist against the atomic and rocket aggression. The great intellectuals and humanists are already striving after establishing peace in the world. Innumerable creeds, social, political and humanitarian, have sprung up. But they cannot give a lasting security against destructive wars. Science with its so many blessings is still paving the way to destruction. The creeds are clashing against one another, much to the bewilderment of the common man. None of them places men of different climes and countries on a common footing. Religion of course teaches men that they are all children of the same God and therefore they are brethren. And yet for lack of knowledge of the essential unity of all religions men have always quarreled with the outer differences amongst themselves. Kriyayoga teaches man that God is to be discovered in his own body first, concentrating his gaze on the point between his eye-brows.

"ईश्वरः सर्व्वभूतानां हृद्देशेऽर्ज्जुन तिष्ठति" said Shrikrisna in the *Gita*. Once man realizes God within his own body, he automatically realizes Him in others too. His body is the temple where he starts worshipping the Prana which controls the entire physical machinery. Each and everybody has this Prana-Vayu in common and by realizing its mystery through Pranayama, etc., man realizes the Supreme Consciousness that controls the Universe, for it is the same force that impels the individual and the Universe. Thus Kriyayoga will go a great way in bringing about a sense of unity amongst all men and women, and ultimately in bringing about world peace. We are on the threshold of a new era. The immortal teachings of Lahiri Mahashay came for us at the proper moment. Preparations have been going on, and we are surely ahead of a great spiritual resurgence of India and the world.

A part from Rajayoga which is Yoga proper, there are 'Hathayoga', 'Mantrayoga' etc. Much stress should not be given on Hathayoga, for the Yogic processes involved in it have as their consummation only physical development. A sound physique is certainly necessary for Sadhana, but that is not the be-all and end-all of a life of the spirit. Mantrayoga can certainly lead man to success, because through a constant chanting of the Mantras the Susumna is gradually opened up. That is why the words "जपात् सिद्धिर्जपात् सिद्धिर्जपात् सिद्धिर्न संशयः" are very true. But the opening of the Susumna through chanting of the Mantras is an indirect process, although it is easier for the common man. The Yogi makes the Susumna his starting point by taking recourse to different processes of controlling and canalizing the Prana-Vayu through the right path.

The liberality inherent in the Kriyayoga of Shri Shri Lahiri Mahashay places it on a universal footing. A man practicing the teachings of any religion may be initiated into Kriyayoga without the necessity of shaking off his own religious faith. Besides, Kriyayoga may be given to any man having an eagerness for Self-Realization, to whichever caste, creed or country he may belong. Shri Shri Lahiri Mahashay had Abdul Gafur Khan as one of his disciples, and Swami Bhaskarananda Saraswati and Shrimat Balananda Brahmachari were two Saints belonging to other religious paths who received Kriyayoga from Shri Shri Lahiri Mahashay.

The Kriyayoga propounded by Lahiri Mahashay is based on the principles enunciated in the *Shrimadbhagavadgita,* and the *Yogasutra* of the great sage Patanjali. Lahiri Baba gave Yogic interpretations to some 22 famous Shastras including the two above-mentioned ones. They will be duly mentioned at the end of this book. The *Gita*, however, was considered to be the most important. It is a compendium of all kinds of spiritual training.

But, after all, Shastras are the records of spiritual researches conducted by Great Saints. Unless one follows the teachings of the Shastras in practice, one cannot have the experience of the Divine Bliss. That is why the mystery of Dharma has been described in the *Gita* as प्रत्यक्षावगमं, to be realized only by direct experience. Shri Shri Lahiri Mahashay's Kriyayoga leads the Sadhaka to the final goal, each stage unfolding its peculiar effect and thus encouraging the seeker.

As the difficult processes of Rajayoga have been much simplified by the Yogiraj and his Great Master Shri Shri Babaji Maharaj, the Kriyayoga as propounded by them has been called the 'Sahaja Kriyayoga' that is, the Kriya that comes naturally to man, without putting any artificial strain on the physical machinery. This, again, is another point in favor of Kriyayoga that it is free from the dangers which sometimes come in the way of the Sadhaka in the shape of some physical distortion or disease, the outcome of mistakes in following the processes of Yoga. There is no such danger attending Kriyayoga even if one commits a mistake. Of course,

Kriyayoga is 'Sahaja' (meaning literally 'that which originates at our very birth') also in the primary sense that it is a process where we have to take recourse to the regulation of breath, the process of inhalation and exhalation which is co-eval with the very being of man.

The advent of Lahiri Mahashay had thus a great significance for suffering humanity, offering as he did, a divine manna to the care-worn earth. Let us, in the next chapter, try to start with a brief account of his Life Divine, which can only be done through His Grace.

CHAPTER II

Early Life: Before Diksa[1]

Shri Shri Shyama Charan Lahiri Mahashay was born on the 16th of Ashwin, 1235 Bengali Era, (1828 A.D.) at the village Ghurni in the district of Nadia in Bengal. His birthdate was not at first exactly known. It was, however, discovered after much research and inquiry into the diaries of the Yogiraj by his grandsons Acharya Sj. Anandamohan Lahiri and Sj. Abhoy Charan Lahiri. It was their family tradition to burn the horoscope after the death of a man. We have, therefore, no horoscope of the Yogiraj. Sj. Abhoy Charan Lahiri, however, had one prepared by Pandit Shri Yageshwar Pathak, a Maharastrian astrologer at Benares. From this also it is evident that the boy would be a great saviour of the suffering humanity. The father of Shri Shri Lahiri Mahashay was Sj. Gourmohan Lahiri Sarkar, the famous landlord of Ghurni, and his mother was Shrimati Muktakeshi Devi, the second wife of Sj. Gourmohan.

The origin of the Lahiri family is to be sought as far back as the great sage Shandilya, the author of *Bhaktisutra* and *Yogasutra.* In Bengal the history of the family is to be traced from Yogiraj Bhattanarayana[2] who came over to Bengal from Kanyakubja (the present Kanpur) with four other sages at the request of Adishur, the then King of Bengal. Thus, it seems, there was a latent tradition of Yoga in the family of Yogiraj Shri Shri Shyama Charan Lahiri Mahashay which was hinted at by Mahavatar Shri Shri Babaji Maharaj after his Diksa[3].

One of the thirteenth descendants from Bhattanarayana, Joysagar by name, was the originator of the Barendra Brahmins. At the arrangement of Ballal Sen the famous King of the Sen dynasty of Bengal, the tract of land at the north of the River Padma and in between the Karatoya and Kushi was called Rajsahi Barendra Bhum ('Bhumi' land). It was because Joysagar settled in this land

1. Initiation.

2. The ancestry of Rabindranath Tagore, too, goes back to Bhattanarayana.

3. Mentioned in Chapter III.

that his family came to be known as Barendra Brahmins. The family of Yogiraj Shri Shri Shyama Charan Lahiri Mahashay was also know as the Lahiris of Nakair, as Keshava the twenty-first person from Bhattanarayana settled in the village Nakair.

The surname Lahiri came to be attached to the family after they received a village named Lahiri in the district of Bagura from the hands of the king at the time of Sj. Pitambar Sharma. The surname was used first by Sj. Lokenath Lahiri, son of Pitambar.

The thirtieth descendant from Bhattanarayana was Thakur Durgadas Lahiri, an inhabitant of the village Halsa near Rajsahi, who inherited the estates of Kalagachhia near Murshidabad after the death of his father-in-law Raja Shambhuchandra Roy who had no other issue excepting the wife of Durgadas. One of the sons of Thakur Durgadas Lahiri was Shrihari who became a Dewan of the then reigning Nabab and received the title Sarkar. Henceforth his descendants used the surname Lahiri Sarkar. Yogiraj Shyama Charan, however, did not use the title Sarkar.

Due to some clash with the Natore Raj family, Sj. Ramballabh Lahiri Sarkar lost the Kalagachhia estates and came over to Krisnanagore in the district of Nadia at the shelter of Raja Raghuram Roy where he became a courtier. It is said that Ramballabh on horseback gave a round over his selected plot of land and thus he received it from the Raja. From this round ('Ghuran' in Bengali) the name of the village became 'Ghurni'. Ramballabh's son Sj. Shibcharan Lahiri Sarkar was the grandfather of the Yogiraj. He was a great artist and the originator of the famous clay-models of Ghurni.

The only purpose of going into this complicated genealogy of the Lahiri family is to show that our Yogiraj was born in a family which was rich in both spiritual and material acquisitions. And this certainly gave his character an aristocracy of its own, a natural gravity and independence of spirit. The constant change of place from Kanauj to Kashi (Benares) where the family settled in the childhood of Shri Shyama Charan may also be an indication of the fact that the spirit of man has no limitations of space and time, that although the birthplace of a man is hallowed by sacred memories, the Yogi has his home in all climes and places. As Tagore has sung: "I have my home everywhere and yet I am seeking for that, alas."

The family tradition, therefore, made it eminently possible that one of the great Yogis of modern India would be born here[1].

Shri Shyama Charan's father Sj. Gourmohan was a great devotee of Lord Shiva and he established a Shiva Temple in his village. The temple, however, was completely washed away by a great flood of the River Jalangi or Khore by the side of which the village Ghurni was situated. The flood also destroyed the house and most of the estates of Gourmohan in the early childhood of Shri Shyama Charan. After this flood-havoc Gourmohan finally settled at Benares where he already had a temporary residence. His eldest son Chandrakanta was at that time living at Benares. It is said that some time after the flood, a woman in the village in her dream was told by Lord Shiva about the exact location where his image was drowned. At her words, people in the village searched out the holy image and installed it in a new temple built for the purpose. The place even now goes by the name of Shibtala at Ghurni.

It is very significant that Lahiri Baba was born in the district of Nadia where a few hundred years back Mahaprabhu Shri Gouranga appeared with his grand message of universal love. The house of Shri Gouranga, too, has gone completely under the water of the Jalangi, a branch of the Ganga. The spiritual glory of these Saints is what is immortal. What they had in the shape of material possessions have gone the way of impermanence. Is it again an indication given to the world about the vanity of all earthly things?

Sj. Gourmohan was a virtuous man who read the *Rigveda* everyday. At Benares he engaged Nagabhatta, a great Vedic scholar, as a tutor to Shri Shyama Charan. The Vedic simplicity and austerity in the character of Lahiri Mahashay was therefore as much inherited as acquired.

The child Shyama Charan was, strangely enough, not at all restless like other boys of his own age. He would often come unnoticed to the riverside and meditate with closed eyes in a lotus posture. He would also sink neck-deep into the sand of the riverside so that his mother might not easily take him home. The women in the

1. Anybody interested in the detailed genealogical table of the Yogiraj family may kindly consult the biographies of the Yogiraj written by Sj. Anandamohan and Sj. Abhoy Charan Lahiri.

neighborhood would compare him with the Yogishwara Lord Shiva at such moments of meditation.

Mrinmayi Devi, Gourmohan's first wife, died on the way to some holy pilgrimage. She had two sons, Chandrakanta and Saradaprasad, and a daughter named Swarnamayi. Gourmohan's second wife Shrimati Muktakeshi Devi had Shyama Charan as her only son and Sulaksana Devi as her only daughter.

It was in 1237 B.S.[1] that the flood destroyed the house of Gourmohan and also the Shiva temple established by him. On Baishakh 19, 1238, however, he established three Shiva-temples at 49 Ganesh Mahalla, Benares. The devotion to Shiva who is taken as the greatest master of the Yogis did not go unrewarded, as we find that the great Yogi Shyama Charan was called the 'Living Vishwanatha'[2] in his later life by the people of Benares, the city of Lord Vishwanatha. Shyama Charan's mother, too, was a pious lady who did not take a single morsel of food before worshipping Shiva everyday.

On Agrahayana 2, 1238 B.S., Gourmohan came to Benares with his family. On Bhadra 4, 1239 B.S., he went to Ghurni for the last time. On Pous 13, 1240, he left with the entire family for Benares where he reached on Falgun 18 (1834 A.D.). Henceforward, he settled permanently at Benares. For some five years the family lived in different parts of the city. At last, in 1245 B.S., Radhanath, the nephew of Gourmohan, purchased the house No. D/32/242 at Madanpura. It was at this house the major portion of the student life of Shri Shyama Charan was spent. The house exists even now.

The first lessons of Yogiraj Shyama Charan started at a 'Pathashala' (a primary school where only elementary lessons are given) at a place called Telibari near the Garureshwar Shiva temple at Benares where he used to go in company with his cousin Shashi. Next he went to the Joynarayan School established by Joynarayan Ghosal, the Zamindar of Bhukailas, in 1818. Gourmohan was liberal enough to understand the value of English education in modern times. In the Joynarayan School however, Hinduism was unnecessarily condemned by some of the Christian Missionaries and

---

1. B.S. : Bengali 'Sal', i.e., Bengali Era.

2. Vishwanatha is just another name for Shiva. It means the 'Lord of the Universe'.

attempts were made to convert the students into Christianity. However, at the age of twelve Shri Shyama Charan left this school and joined the English school under the Government Sanskrit College, Benares. Here he learned English, Hindi, Urdu and some Persian. Bengali he had to learn at home. Bengali was not a compulsory subject in schools at Benares and that explains the Hindi writings in his diaries in the Bengali script.

The first lessons the Yogiraj learned in Sanskrit were learned from his father himself. After that Gourmohan appointed Nagabhatta, a Marathi tutor, who was well versed in the Shastras. Shyama Charan studied the *Rigveda*, the *Upanisads* and other scriptures with him.

The English school where Shri Shyama Charan used to read was later converted into a College affiliated under Cambridge University. Shyama Charan left the College in 1848. We have no means of knowing whether he passed the Junior or Senior Scholarship Examination there. Sj. Abhoy Charan Lahiri, however, has informed us in his book of a certificate given by the English Headmaster to Shri Shyama Charan. We reproduce below the certificate as printed in the book of Sj. Abhoy Charan.

GOVERNMENT COLLEGE
BENARES

This is to certify that Shamacharan Lahiree age about 19 years old, the son of Gourmohan Lahiree, inhabitant of Zilla Benares, has attended the College for eight years, during which he has afforded very great satisfaction to his teachers by his good disposition, exemplary conduct, regularity in attendance and diligence in the prosecution of his studies.

He possesses a very good knowledge of English, composes letters and translates from English into Urdu and vice versa with considerable facility and correctness and is tolerably acquainted with Literature, History and Geography.

He has gained several prizes during the time he has been in the Institution.

Benares.
26 July 1848.

Sd/-Geo. Nicholls
Headmaster, Benares College

Apart from his College studies Shyama Charan would also take English, Persian and other books regularly from the College Library and note such portions from them as would appeal to his mind. This practice shows Shyama Charan's all-absorbing devotion to studies, so rare in these days amongst students. It reveals also the fact that from his very boyhood whatever Shyama Charan did he did with all his heart. It is this concentration, this taking a thing in all sincerity, that is the greatest prerequisite for a Yogi. And the boy Shyama Charan had the makings of a Yogiraj from the very start of his life.

His education, however, was never cut off from the basis of spirituality. Apart from the Vedic and the Philosophic studies with Nagabhatta, Shri Shyama Charan would, under the instructions from his father, go to Shri Shri Kedarnath after finishing his daily Vedic Chant, and would perform his daily prayer by the side of the Holy Ganga. Incidentally it may be mentioned that a riverside has always been considered a suitable place for Sadhana by sages like Manu. Thus we find that the materialistic education in our schools and colleges would be too feeble to destroy the core of spirituality deep down in the heart of Shri Shyama Charan.

As is also evident from the Headmaster's Certificate, Shyama Charan was very regular and punctual in his attendance at the school. He would generally go to school after a very slender meal of rice with a touch of 'Ghee' and salt. Coming back from the school in the afternoon he would sit silent for some time at his reading table. The tiffin at that time was grams and molasses. But if on any occasion the tiffin would be forgotten by the members of the family, he would never ask for it. After an hour he would start for the temple of Shri Shri Kedarnath. It is very surprising that even the boy Shyama Charan did not have the habit of asking for anything, be it his legitimate due. A complete lack of attachment to his meals and dresses and other human wants was a very natural and spontaneous virtue with him. He would only accept what came for him, unasked. Thus, even when salt was lacking in his curry, he would never want it. If, afterwards, the cook would be ashamed on finding out his mistake, Shyama Charan would make light of the affair with some such remark as "A single day's mistake doesn't matter at all". Regarding dress, too, he was supremely careless and would never want a cloth even if he would have to use a torn and worn-out one while going to school. It was only when the family authorities would look to the matter that a new cloth would be purchased. Apart from his lack of avarice and at attachment this also shows the great dignity and real aristocracy of Shyama Charan's mind which did not feel the necessity of being a suitor for ordinary wants.

Shri Shyama Charan had great physical strength and he could also stand hard labor. His adventurous spirit is revealed in his boyhood habit of taking a plunge and swimming over the Ganga from Gouranga Ghat (or Goren Ghat) to Kedar Ghat and back again from Kedar Ghat against the strong current of the rainy season. He would not indulge in idle talks with his companions, and although generous, had such a dignity and gravity about himself that his companions always obeyed him as their leader. Besides, his keen intelligence and power of judgment was a guide to them all. And naturally, his friends, too, would be inspired to give a good account of themselves in life.

It is palpable from the above that Shri Shyama Charan had every quality, even as a boy, that has been extolled by our Shastras. Indeed, it is the Shastras which follow the sages and not the sages who have to follow the Shastric injunctions. They come to them naturally and spontaneously, without any strain or effort on their part to acquire them. The 'Yogavatar' (the Divine as the embodiment of Yoga) came to instruct the world, to teach men how to remove their sufferings, and therefore, it was in the fitness of things that the Divine descended on him with an easy grace of Perfection.

According to the custom prevalent at that time Shyama Charan was married early at the age of eighteen. His father-in-law, Sj. Debnarayan Sanyal Vachaspati, was a reputed scholar as the very title 'Vachaspati' (Master of Scriptures) denotes. Before settling at Khalispura Mahalla at Benares Vachaspati Mahashay was a resident of Belur in the district of Howrah, Bengal. He was a very religious man and used frequently to go to Gourmohan's house where he read and discussed the *Upanisads* and other scriptures. Vachaspati was a widower and had to bring up three sons and a daughter. The youngest child, the daughter Kashimoni, was very favorite with her father. She would very often come with him to the house of Gourmohan and the boy Shyama Charan was her playmate there. Sometimes the elderly ladies of the house would humorously ask the young girl, "whom would you marry, dear"? And Kashimoni at once pointed out the gentle fair-complexioned Shyama Charan. It may be noted, incidentally, that Kashimoni herself was not of a very bright complexion.

However, Kashimoni Devi was married to Shyama Charan at the tender age of nine. Since then, she always stood by her husband through thick and thin, through all sorts of household troubles and duties and monetary want. It was through her patient efforts that the household of the Yogiraj was always efficiently managed, and a house too could be built from the slender income of Shyama Charan. Kashimoni was always true to the ideals of a Hindu wife in her great devotion to her husband, in her modesty and her sympathy with the distressed. Even in her old age she would herself give alms to the first beggar every morning in her household, and then the other members would take up the job. She was convinced that the suffering and the distressed were so many images of God blessing the house by accepting service from its members.

This worthy consort of Shri Shyama Charan was initiated into Kriyayoga by her illustrious husband and reached a highly advanced stage in the world of spirit. Her grandson Abhoy Charan notes in his book that he saw her once in a state of Samadhi or complete spiritual absorption. Kashimoni Devi died at the age of 94 in the month of Chaitra, 1337 B.S. She retained full consciousness even up to the moment of her death.

In his married life the Yogiraj had lost a few children up to the year 1852. At about this time the atmosphere in the joint family came to be disturbed due to difference of opinions amongst cousin brothers. Lahiri Mahashay shifted with his family to a house near about at Simonchowhatta.

In December, 1863, Shri Shri Lahiri Mahashay went to Krisnanagore in order to make arrangements for 288 bighas of land which he inherited from his father and which were so long unlawfully occupied by his relatives. As it was almost impossible to enjoy his rights over the land from as distant a place as Benares, Lahiri Mahashay made over the property to the same relatives on condition that they would send him some rent regularly. As soon as he turned toward Benares, however, his relatives conveniently forgot the promise and thus Lahiri Mahashay lost his landed property altogether. Was this a sign that for the future Yogiraj such material acquisitions were of a very secondary importance? Does it not show again the fact that riches very often are sources of troubles than an advantage in the path of spiritual progress? The spiritualist should also know that he cannot depend ever upon the nearest relations who may only seek for the betrayal of his interests, that his only friend and relative is 'Atman', the Soul Supreme. All this, therefore, leads one's mind to non-attachment to material possessions.

But, after all, the Yogiraj had adopted a householder's life and he had duties to his wife and children. There also we find him dutiful in every aspect of family life. He earned money by honest-efforts and would always fight shy of being a suitor for anything which was not his legitimate share. Thus he synthesized in himself the seemingly contradictory duties of a householder and a spiritual master.

Shri Shri Lahiri Mahashay had two sons, Shri Shri Tinkori Lahiri born in 1863 and Shri Shri Dukori Lahiri born in 1865. Both attained to great spiritual eminence in their lives. The late Acharya Anandamohan Lahiri, the first biographer of the Yogiraj, was the son of Shri Shri Dukori Lahiri Mahashay. Another biographer of Shri Shri Lahiri Mahashay is found in Sj. Abhoy Charan Lahiri, son of Shri Shri Tinkori Lahiri Mahashay.

Shri Shri Tinkori Lahiri Mahashay
(Eldest son of the Yogiraj)

Shrimati Kashimoni Devi – Wife of the Yogiraj

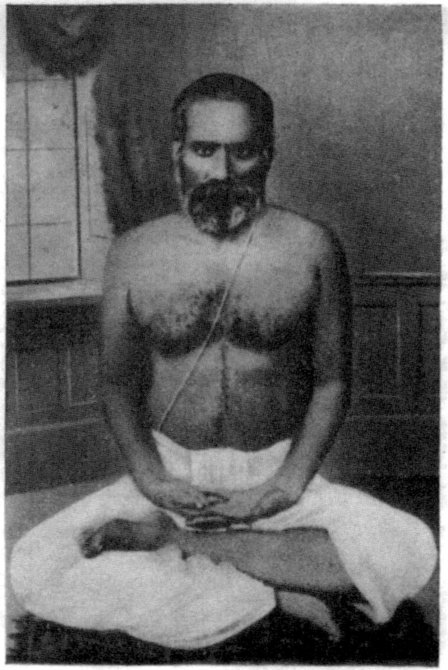

Shri Shri Dukori Lahiri Mahashay
(Younger son of the Yogiraj)

CHAPTER III

Diksa or Initiation.

Shri Shri Lahiri Mahashay lost his father on May 31, 1852 A.D., Jyaistha 20, Tuesday, 1259 B.S. A few years before that, on September 1, 1849[1], he entered the Military Works Branch, P.W.D., Benares Division as a second clerk. The office at that time was at Gajipur. This department had the duty of supplying materials for the army and building roads. At this time Shri Shri Lahiri Mahashay had also to teach Hindi, Urdu and Bengali to Engineers and other officers of his department. Throughout his service life he had a very good reputation for his honesty, efficiency, and sense of responsibility as witness the certificates from all the officers under whom he had worked. In his service life the Yogiraj was promoted up to the post of a Barrack-master, which was equivalent to that of the modern S.D.O. of the Public Works Department.

It was in 1861[2] that Lahiri Mahashay got the order to transfer to Ranikhet, a forest region near Nainital in the Himalayas. He was then working in the office at Benares[3]. The Government wanted to establish a military cantonment at Ranikhet and for this purpose the P.W.D. Military Works Branch was ordered to clear off the jungles and to prepare a level ground. Captain G. Burney was appointed the Executive Engineer at the Ranikhet Division.

Situated at an altitude of about 6000 feet and surrounded on all sides by forest-girdled mountains, Ranikhet has actually been a favorite haunt for Yogis. When, however, the cantonment was going to be established, the Sadhus retired to lonelier places. A few of them remained, evidently in order to establish a contact divine with

---

1. Sj. Anandamohan Lahiri Mahashay gives us the approximate date of 1851. Here we have depended on the later account given by Sj. Abhoy Charan Lahiri Mahashay.

2. In 1868, according to Sj. Abhoy Charan Lahiri Mahashay who claims to have possessed some of the diaries and other documents of the Yogiraj.

3. According to Sj. Anandamohan, Shri Shri Lahiri Mahashay was working as the second clerk in the Assist. Commanders Royal Engineering Office at Danapur, just before his transfer to Ranikhet.

the mortal world, a contact which was to bless us anew with the occult mysteries of Yoga.

It was at Ranikhet that the most significant event in the life of Shri Shri Lahiri Mahashay took place. It was here that he received the Blessed Touch of his Master under whose benign influence he became the greatest exponent of the Yoga teachings in modern times.

There are different and conflicting accounts regarding the meeting of the Yogiraj with his Master Shri Shri Babaji Maharaj, and his initiation. The conflict seems to be between the spirit which claims to start from a rational and scientific basis and rejects all improbable incidents as entirely unbelievable, and that which blindly accepts everything – facts and legends, however improbable and fantastic – as gospel truth the validity of which cannot simply be questioned. The truth seems to stand midway between these two extremes. While accepting on the whole the point of view of the so-called rationalist in weighing the available data so as to see how much of them can stand the test of reason, it is impossible while dealing with the life of a spiritualist par excellence to reject all that seems to be fantastic to the ordinary human understanding. For, in matters of the Divine, reason fails and recoils at the vision of the Transcendent Glory. How can rationality be able to grasp that which is Supra-Rational by its very nature? It is for this reason that Brahman has been called "अवाङ्मनसगोचरम्" in the *Upanisads*. Reason on the mental plane of human consciousness reels and staggers until it is completely silenced in the presence of the Supra-mental Reality. It is not that everything about the Supreme Reality is unscientific, only because it is Intuition rather than Intellect that leads towards the Divine. The Supreme Reality is, on the other hand, the only perfect scientific phenomenon in the Universe. Only it does not always tally with our day-to-day science which is a very imperfect imitation of Super-Reason. The Divine is the greatest scientist as well as the greatest artist. It is the Supreme Reconciliation and Synthesis of all seeming opposites and therefore combines rationality with intuition. It is only here that there is no distinction between the 'Jnanin' and the 'Bhakta'. If, therefore, we come across some highly improbable events in the life divine of Shri Shri Lahiri Mahashay, we should not at once feel tempted to reject them outright. As the greatest portion of spirituality is Revealed Knowledge, we would perhaps do well to accept such accounts as might have come from some of the greatest disciples of the Yogiraj even where the facts are not available.

Although, however, there are differences in details of how exactly the Yogiraj received his first initiation, what is important for us and for the world too is to note that the initiation brought about a silent revolution (or evolution, if one likes) in the life of Shri Shri Lahiri Mahashay and paved the way for a regeneration of human consciousness which must ultimately bring about a new world-order for a more spiritually enlightened age.

As the office work at Ranikhet was not at all heavy, Shyama Charan had ample time to move about in the vast grandeur of the Himalayas. It was really a very beautiful place. On all sides there were vast mountain ranges through which the River Gaugus was flowing. At some distance there was the Dwarahat Hill and just above it was the Dronagiri or Dhunagiri. The distance between Ranikhet and Dronagiri was only 15 miles.

One afternoon Shri Shri Lahiri Mahashay went deep into the nearabout forest. The darkness of evening was fast descending. Shri Shyama Charan was absorbed in the beauty of Nature. Of a sudden came a call, "Shyama Charan, you've come!" Shyama Charan was highly surprised by hearing his name uttered by a Sadhu with whom he had no acquaintance. Doubts arose in his mind whether he had fallen in the hands of a cheat. But the Sadhu knew the thoughts of his mind and gradually gave him details of his ancestry. Doubts however, still continued in the mind of Shri Shri Lahiri Mahashay. The holy man told him that he was not a deceiver and asked Shyama Charan whether he could remember if he had came there before. Shri Shri Lahiri Mahashay repeatedly answered in the negative. The Sannyasi drew Shyama Charan's attention to a few equipments of a mendicant which were lying aside in a cave, a Stick ('Danda') and Waterpot ('Kamandalu') a Tigerskin and Fireplace etc. But still Shri Shri Lahiri Baba could not recall his association with them. At last the mysterious Sadhu touched the head of Shyama Charan, and lo! an electric current passed as it were through his entire body. The cave as well as the things there suddenly seemed to be very familiar to Shri Shyama Charan. The Holy Man narrated that Shri Shyama Charan was his disciple in his former birth when he used to meditate in this very cave, and the equipments were really his own. It was his Gurudeva who brought him here by his spiritual force. The telegram transferring Shri Shri Lahiri Mahashay to Ranikhet was only a mistake on the part of the authorities. Within a week again he would be ordered back to his former place. "The Office was brought here for you, and not you for the Office", said the Great Saint.

That single Blessed Touch was sufficient for Shyama Charan to revive all the wealth of his former spiritual glory. He did not have the mind now to come back to his household life and prayed earnestly to stay with his Master. But the Master did not agree, as Shyama Charan was the Man of Destiny to fulfill the mission of propagating the lost secrets of Yoga (as described in the *Gita*) to the world at large, particularly to the householders. Lord Shrikrisna revived the Yoga which was almost forgotten with the passage of time and gave it to Arjuna, his fit disciple. The age came for another revival and Shri Shri Babaji Maharaj let the mantle of the missionary fall on the shoulders of mundane affairs. Besides, one of the most ancient exponents of Yoga was the great sage Shandilya in whose family Shri Shri Lahiri Mahashay was born. The *Shandilya Upanisad* was even older than the *Yogasutra* of Patanjali. That was why Shri Shri Babaji Maharaj told the Yogiraj that the Kriyayoga in which he was being initiated was actually a possession of their own.

Everyday after this fateful meeting Shri Shri Lahiri Mahashay used to go to his great Gurudeva and spend some hours in his elevating company. He also used to take his meals prepared under the instruction of his Master. One day it so happened that Shri Shri Babaji Maharaj asked Shyama Charan to take a potful of Castor Oil as his only food and drink. There were of course hesitations in the mind of Shri Shyama Charan, but nevertheless he carried out the instruction and, according to the will of his Master lay down on the bank of the River Gaugus. This hill stream had a very strong current which bore him far away. He was almost senseless due to an attack of Cholera as an aftermath of taking the Castor Oil.

The next day, Shri Shri Babaji Maharaj told Shyama Charan, that the purgation had a very wholesome effect on him, as it purged away all the physical ills that might stand in the way of his grand spiritual illumination. Now he was given a sumptuous repast of

'Luchi' and Halua'. The same evening was chosen for Shri Shyama Charan's initiation.

In the evening Shri Shri Lahiri Mahashay had to be prepared for a miracle. Following his great Master, he entered a palace which seemed to be a material embodiment of a fairy-tale grandeur. There was an almost unbelievable magnificence of decoration, furniture, and servants male and female. There were also arrangements for a grand feast. The same night Shri Shyama Charan and another devotee were given initiation by Shri Shri Babaji Maharaj. One of the greatest spiritual dramas in modern times was thus enacted in complete silence amidst the vast Himalayas, the land of the Yogis. Does it show the eternal truth that the greatest conquest, viz., the conquest of one's own self, always fights shy of the clamor of public gaze and is performed in golden silence?

The next morning, however, to his utter surprise, Shri Shyama Charan found no trace of the gorgeous palace. In its place stood the good old cave of his Guruji before him. As Shri Shri Babaji Maharaj later explained, a great Yogi can at will take some atoms from the air and make them condensed into any shape he likes. Again, after its function was over, the shape would be dissolved "into air, into thin air" at his will. This may at first seem to be completely fictitious, but the Yogi knows that it is perfectly scientific. Everything in this world is made up of atoms assuming a particular shape. The Yogi knows the secret of atoms as he is in unison with the "One Spirit" which "impels all" atoms and is one with each of them. Hence this Prospero-like trick is entirely at the disposal of a Yogi. The difference of Yoga from magic, however, is this, that the former is all-powerful and devoid of any merely mundane purpose. Shri Shri Lahiri Mahashay in his former birth had the desire to live in such a palace just for a day and it was now fulfilled by the grace of his Shriguru. Not that Shri Shyama Charan had any attachment to riches and gorgeousness. Such a desire would just enable him to come again here in this world, because complete lack of desires stops one's cycle of birth and death. But how could that be? After all, Shri Shyama Charan was the chosen pathmaker of Yoga in modern times. His desire was just like that of Shri Ramakrisna who sometimes used to take a great quantity of sweets just in order to avoid a constant Samadhi.

Mahavatar Shri Shri Babaji Maharaj

That Shri Shri Lahiri Mahashay had already achieved his spiritual consummation in his former birth and regained his mortal existence just in order to fulfill the Divine mission of propagating Yoga amongst the masses ("लोकसंग्रहार्थम्" as described in the *Gita*) also proved by the fact that he learned all the complicated processes of Rajayoga only within a week. Ordinarily consummation in Yoga is reached after a life-long Sadhana for many births. That consummation can only come to a man within seven days when his Sadhana has already been complete in some former existence.

As the *Gita* tells us:
"पूर्वाभ्यासेन तेनैव ह्रियते ह्यवशोऽपि सः ।
जिज्ञासुरपि योगस्य शब्दब्रह्मातिवर्तते ॥"

The practice of Yoga in former lives leads the Yogi automatically to a detachment from earthly pleasures. He can attain a greater success than is declared in the Vedas for virtuous deeds, even if he merely inquires into the secrets of Yoga. The Sadhana of Shri Shri Lahiri Mahashay was ready to bear fruit. And his latent faculties woke up at the Blessed Touch of his great Shriguru. Just after his Diksa he remained locked in Nirvikalpa Samadhi (the highest state of absorption in the Divine)[1] for seven days at a stretch.

We do not know the exact name of Shri Shyama Charan's spiritual Master, but he is generally referred to as Babaji or the Father. Who else can be properly described as a Father than one who leads the erring children of this earth into the life divine, the only life which is real and knows no death or sorrow? But Shri Shri Babaji Maharaj was also known as the 'Tryambaka Baba' (one who has three eyes, including the 'Jnana-Netra' or the eye of Divine Knowledge the seat of which, according to Yogis, is in between the eyebrows) or 'Shiva Baba' after the name of Lord Shiva who is regarded as "Yogishwara' or the Master Yogi.

Next to nothing is known regarding the life of Shri Shri Babaji Maharaj, and Mahayogis like him are generally far off from the contact of ordinary mortals. Besides, it was not the custom of Shri Shri Babaji to stay for a long time in any particular place. After

1. In this state the bodily functions are totally suspended and the consciousness of the Sadhaka has no seperate existence whatsoever.

a few days he would generally order his devotees to move with their equipment to a new place with the watchwords "Dera danda uthao" – "raise the shelter and stick (to move with them elsewhere)". It is said that he was many hundred years old and initiated the great Shankaracharya in the Yoga path. He was also the spiritual preceptor of Sadhu Haridas. But although Babaji Maharaj was very old, he possessed eternal youth, because after every hundred years or so he would renew his body with the 'Kayabyuha-Yoga', a process which can be practiced only by the greatest Yogis. The disciples of Shri Shri Lahiri Mahashay who had seen him were all of the opinion that the physical features of Shri Shri Babaji Maharaj were almost like those of his favorite disciple Shri Shyama Charan. Only Shyama Charan looked much older than his Gurudeva who could almost be taken as the former's son. But, again, Babaji never appeared twice in the same form although his similarity with his disciple was a common feature in every case. This perhaps leads towards the conclusion that for Shri Shri Babaji Maharaj who is all spirit, and can assume any form at will, bodily considerations are entirely beside the point and therefore he would just assume a form similar to his beloved Shyama Charan when he would have to appear before the disciples of Shri Shri Lahiri Baba. Besides, the devotees of Shri Shyama Charan had a great devotion to their Gurudeva, and as such they would very much like and revere the appearance of the Paramgurudeva (the guru of Shri Gurudeva) in a form similar to that of their beloved Master. There might have been another reason for the different forms which Shri Shri Babaji Maharaj assumed at different times. It also helped to keep his physical identity hidden from the view of others.

Shri Shyama Charan had been the witness of a few interesting events at the Dronagiri. It is said that the Pandavas of the *Mahabharata* lived here for some time with their preceptor Dronacharya after whose name the place is so called. There was a temple on the Dronagiri, some four or five miles away from the cave of Shri Shyama Charan. The temple was visited every midnight by a Sadhu with a halo of resplendent light round his figure which could be seen from a great distance. The mysterious man would stay a little within the temple and then go away. Nobody would disturb him at that time by going to the temple. Shri Shri

Babaji Maharaj described him as Shri Ashwatthama, son of Shri Dronacharya of the *Mahabharata.*[1]

Dronagiri of course was full of various medicinal plants, but apart from that, if any diseased man would take shelter on the hill visited by Shri Ashwatthama, depending solely on his Grace, he would really be cured of his indisposition. It so happened that a hungry disciple of Shri Shri Babaji Maharaj one day took some poisonous fruits by mistake. Babaji Maharaj had already cautioned many of his disciples against that fruit. However, in the absence of Shri Shri Babaji Maharaj, Shri Shyama Charan and his spiritual companions were at first at a loss as to what to do. The deadly poison had its effect on the man in the form of Cholera and made him completely disfigured. After much deliberation they were suddenly reminded of the Grace of Ashwatthama as related by Shri Shri Babaji Maharaj himself. They carried the patient along and laid him down on the road leading to the temple. The next day the man came back completely recovered and narrated his experience. At midnight the great Sadhu with the halo of divine light came and on seeing him on the road, thundered "Who are you"? After that he just kicked the patient twice which made him fall down on a much lower surface of the hill. Strangely enough, however, the diseased man felt renovated and free from disease as soon as he fell down. After this he could only hear the sounds of opening and closing the temple door. Early at dawn he could also notice the halo again taking its leave from the hill.

Many of the disciples of Shri Shri Babaji Maharaj were highly advanced Yogis and could utilize their prowess for the good of others when it became essential. On one occasion Shri Shyama Charan and some of his spiritual brothers went to the opposite banks of the river nearby. At that time the hill stream did not have much water and as such they could easily cross it walking. On their return journey, however, they found the stream in flow-tide with a very strong current. What could they do now? Of a sudden, one of the foremost disciples of Shri Shri Babaji Maharaj took off his turban which was 10 1/2 yards long. There were seven persons in the company. He just tied seven knots in the turban, threw it into the river and asked his brothers to keep tight each to a single knot. He

1. Here it should be noted in passing that Ashwatthama is one of those who have been gifted with a never-ending life.

himself infused strength in the turban so that it might easily be kept afloat. Thus, with the help of the turban all were safe on the other side of the river. This was just an example of the immense power reached by the Yogis in India. Such miraculous power is called 'Bibhuti' which is generally sub-divided into eight groups: – 'Anima' or the power of making oneself as small as an atom; 'Laghima' or the power of becoming lighter than air; 'Byapti' or the power of spreading oneself over the entire Universe; 'Prakamya' or the power to acquire anything at the mere wish; 'Mahima' or the power to assume any shape; 'Ishitwa' or the control over the beings of the Universe; 'Bashitwa' or the power to move everywhere; and 'Kamavasayita' or the power to stay at any place. But although these Bibhutis came automatically to a Sadhaka as he advances in his Sadhana, misuse of them may lead him far from the goal which is complete Self-Realization. The proper attitude towards these powers should be, as the sages tell us, neither that of pride nor that of hatred. They should be accepted in all humility as the kind gifts of God to one who takes shelter under His Grace.

Although the Kriyayoga has been made simple and rather easily available through the grace of Shri Shri Lahiri Mahashay, Shri Shri Babaji Maharaj would sometimes set very hard tests before initiating one into the path. Shri Shri Lahiri Mahashay would often tell his own disciples incidents from the life of his great Master showing thereby the rareness of the gift with which they had been blessed. One should not, therefore, neglect such a rare possession due to idleness and indecision. A very old Sannyasi, as the Yogiraj related, lived for a long time near the cave of Shri Shri Babaji Maharaj and served his disciples with the expectation to receive initiation from him. One day he prayed very earnestly for Diksa. When Shri Shri Babaji Maharaj did not agree, the old man resolved to die unless he would get it. The Great Babaji just said, "Then die, if life has become so cheap for you". The Sannyasi actually jumped from the hills and died. The Gracious Babaji Maharaj then took up his body, revived him by the power of his Yoga and gave him initiation in his new life.

As a matter of fact Shri Shri Babaji Maharaj was the perfect pattern of greatness which is always "वज्रादपि कठोराणि, मृदूनि कुसुमादपि", i.e., hard and resolute like thunder and at the same time as soft at heart as a delicate flower. His cruelty or callousness was just another name for his Grace, for whenever he tested a man it was only for the latter's well-being. This explains his rudeness sometimes on his disciples in beating them with the burning brands of his holy fire. In general, however, Shri Shri Babaji Maharaj was always amiable and full of humor.

A rich businessman once invited Shri Shri Babaji Maharaj to grace his house by attending a dinner on the occasion of a festival Babaji Maharaj accepted his invitation and told him that he would go with Shri Shyama Charan rather early and would take his meal before all others. On the fixed date he reached there with Shri Shyama Charan and was received very cordially by the householder. But at the dinner came a miracle. The holy man devoured up all the delicacies arranged for the guests and demanded more. The businessman was at his wit's end. Shri Shri Lahiri Mahashay prayed to his Shriguru to spare the man. Babaji replied that the man had great pride for his riches although his resources were limited, as all human resources must necessarily be.

However, the blessed days for Shri Shri Lahiri Mahashay in company with his Gurudeva were coming to a close. The orders for his transfer came. Before his departure he prayed to his Master for relaxing the rigor in granting initiation in the Kriya. He was for giving it to anybody with earnestness, however imperfect he might be. The Master appreciated his disciples sympathy with the suffering humanity and granted his prayer. He also received the permission to permit others to give initiation.

Before parting from his preceptor Shri Shyama Charan was overwhelmed with grief, but Shri Shri Babaji Maharaj consoled him by saying that he would give 'Darshan' to Shri Shyama Charan whenever he would pray to him. This divine promise, however, gave rise to a very awkward situation later on. While on his way back to Ranikhet Shri Shri Lahiri Mahashay halted at the house of a gentleman. Some Bengalee gentlemen there expressed their doubt as to whether really holy men are available in modern times. Naturally, Shri Shri Lahiri Baba protested and told them that he could show them one of the greatest Sadhus. The curiosity of everybody present was aroused at this and they pressed Shri Shyama Charan for the miraculous show. What could Shri Shri Lahiri Mahashay do? He had to yield to their pressure and he started meditation in a closed room of the house with nobody present by his side. Very soon Shri Shri Babaji Maharaj appeared in a resplendent halo of light. He was true to his promise. But at the same time he sternly rebuked Shri Shyama Charan for calling him on such a flimsy ground for sheer fun and said that henceforward he would not always appear at his disciple's request. Only when he himself would feel it necessary for Shri Shyama Charan, would he grace him with a visit. However, at the earnest request of Shri Shri Lahiri Mahashay he gave Darshan to those waiting outside the room and took 'Halua' for their satisfaction distributing 'prasad' amongst them.

After this incident Shri Shri Babaji Maharaj sometimes visited his disciple of his own accord. The great disciples of Shri Shri Lahiri Mahashay, too, were sometimes graced with his Darshan and given valuable instructions at significant moments in their lives.

The holy communion between Shri Shyama Charan and his great Gurudeva is, however, a lofty spiritual drama which passes the comprehension of us, ordinary mortals. For a great realization of that Divine Comedy one should progress along their path with an untiring devotion and an unflinching faith in their Grace. Then and then alone the Kindly Light will dawn upon one, the light that upholds and illumines, raises and supports.

CHAPTER IV

As an 'Acharya'[1]

While still at Ranikhet, Shri Shri Lahiri Mahashay initiated a few Sadhus in Kriyayoga under the instructions from his Gurudeva. On coming back to the plains, his first disciple was a garland-maker named Yogi who used to sell flowers outside the temple of Lord Kedareshwara near about the Narada Ghat.[2] The next disciple was a cobbler named Bhagavandas (Servant of the Lord!). This shows that Shri Shri Lahiri Mahashay made no distinction of caste, creed, and community in giving initiation. He was really the "भावग्राही जनार्दनः" (the Lord who looks into the heart alone) who could enter into the inmost corner of the human heart and therefore anybody with sincerity and devotion would receive the Grace of Initiation from him, while others would have to be disappointed in spite of their learning and culture and riches. Very often it happened that a so-called educated gentleman would have to wait for years before receiving initiation from him. Some had to go entirely disappointed. This, of course, does not mean that anybody would be deprived of his Grace. His heart was large enough to feel for the well-being of every mortal. Only, the rarest possession of Kriyayoga could not be entrusted in utterly anti-divine hands. This was for the good of the men themselves. Shri Shyama Charan's rejection in regard to initiation would often transform a sinner into a great devotee and then the Master was all Grace to him.

Even Muslims and men of other communities were not deprived of initiation. Thus Abdul Gafu Khan was a highly advanced disciple of Shri Shri Lahiri Mahashay and was given the right to initiate others.

Shri Shyama Charan's sympathy with the poor and the down-trodden was immense. Instead of taking anything from them

1. Preceptor.

2. Is it significant that the name of the flower-dealer was Yogi and the name of the Ghat was after Narada the great devotee of the Lord? Notice the place, too, where he used to take his seat. It was in the vicinity of a temple of Lord Shiva, the greatest exponent of Yoga.

in the shape of money and other presentations, he would rather help them from his own pocket. To receive any material presents, whether from the rich or from the poor, was generally against the principle of the Yogiraj. 'Pratigraha' or receiving gifts was almost a forbidden thing in his family itself and Shri Shyama Charan generally followed this tradition with scrupulous care. He would only take Rupees five at the time of initiating anybody, as he was instructed to do so by Shri Shri Babaji Maharaj. This custom too originated from the fact that a man generally values something only when he has to pay for it. That the divine Kriyayoga should not be misused in the hands of ordinary mortals was the motive force behind the introduction of this custom. Shri Shri Lahiri Mahashay sent these sums to his Gurudeva. Even now-a-days the amount of money thus received is spent in some noble spiritual cause. For the poor and the unable disciple the Yogiraj often paid this 'Guru-daksina' to himself. Besides, this spiritual aristocrat was the real exponent of democracy in its truest form which depends not on quantity but on the quality of the heart. The poor and uneducated disciples of the Yogiraj were equally treated by him with the rich and many of them were regarded and honored as advanced Yogis. Thus the first disciple of Shri Shyama Charan at Danapur was an ordinary peon named Brinda Bhakat. Although without academic education, Brinda had attained such a direct realization of the Infinite that all knowledge was revealed to him through Divine Grace. Once he surprised an assembly of learned scholars at the place of a Zamindar at Bankipore by settling some intricate spiritual disputes among them in very simple words and was rewarded by the landlord. Brinda explained that Yoga embraces all Sadhana within itself. Whenever there is a secret mystery in any Sadhana, the theory of Yoga has been involved. Thus even in the six systems of philosophy, different paths have not been advocated, but only the six different stages of the same Yoga.

Once it so happened that a gentleman who had received initiation from the Yogiraj some time back was pressing him for the grace of second initiation. Just at that moment reached Brinda came into the presence of his Gurudeva. The Master asked him, "Well, Brinda, would you like to have the second initiation?" "Oh, no, Sir," Brinda appealed to his Master, "the very first initiation received from you has so much overwhelmed me that I find it difficult to deliver letters". "Brinda is floating in the Ocean of Sachchidananda",[1] said the Yogiraj.

Another incident has come down to us which reveals the depth of tenderness hidden within the heart of Shri Shri Lahiri Mahashay. The Maharaja of some place, who was a disciple of the Yogiraj, once took him to his house and made all arrangements for his comfort. But Shri Shri Lahiri Baba showed himself rather fastidious in his taste. There was an extremely poor man nearby who earnestly requested the Yogiraj to grace his cottage with his Lotus Feet. Lahiri Mahashay agreed. On arriving there, however, he found that the man prepared a fish curry for him with great devotion. Now the Yogiraj was a complete vegetarian. But he found that if he would not take the curry, it would not be possible for his devotee at that moment to gather and prepare something else for him. He, therefore, took rice with the same fish curry and slept at the house for some time. On his return, the Maharaja who was already informed of this through his attendants asked Shri Shri Lahiri Mahashay about the reason for this differential treatment. He used to arrange high-quality dishes for his Gurudeva and yet the Master would not seem to be satisfied. The Yogiraj, however, replied that behind all his costly arrangements there was always a sense of pride which really caused discomfort to the Master. The poor devotee, on the other hand, was all humility and simplicity before his Master. Everything, therefore, tasted sweet in his house.

However, it is not that Shri Shri Lahiri Mahashay looked only to the poor and his door was closed for the rich; for the rich too might have honesty, simplicity and devotion. As a matter of fact the Grace of Shri Shri Lahiri Mahashay was showered upon all – high and low, mean and elevated, the rich and the poor. Devotion was to him the only passport to the Divine and whosoever had even a modest share of it was graced by him in a concrete form. The Maharaja Ishwarinarayan Sinha of Benares was one of the devoted disciples of Shri Shri Lahiri Mahashay. The Maharaja of Khetri was another.

The unbounded sympathy of the Yogiraj did not keep itself circumscribed within the human world alone. It was also extended to the birds and beasts and all things of the Universe. It was Lahiri Mahashay who moved the Government against shooting down

1. Eternal Existence, Supreme Consciousness and Bliss.

pigeons living happily in the palaces on the bank of the Ganga at Benares, and stopped the cruel practice for ever.

The Yogiraj was not in favor of indiscriminate propaganda for Kriyayoga. He would rather ask his disciples to go on silently with their Sadhana and a time would come, according to him, when the Yoga would be accepted all over the world. In an age when we always tend to talk big and do nothing, it is easily conceivable how wholesome his instruction really is. Indeed, propaganda devoid of the surest basis of sincere action leaves no lasting effect on the human mind. Such propaganda, instead of doing good to people often makes them misunderstand the very spirit of Sadhana. Silent work, on the other hand, produces such strength and conviction in the Sadhaka that he becomes sure of winning his way even through the heaviest odds. Spiritual consummation must first be achieved in one's own life, and then alone it can be spread throughout the world. The prophecy of Shri Shri Lahiri Mahashay, however, on the spreading and propagation of the Kriyayoga has proved true in modern times. Already the message of the Yogiraj has reached America and Europe through Paramhansa Yogananda, the great disciple of Shrimat Swami Shri Yukteshwar Giriji Maharaj who was one of the foremost disciples of Shri Shri Lahiri Mahashay.

The Yogiraj would generally instruct his devotees not to forsake their normal social and religious customs. Persons who had already been initiated by their family preceptors could also practice their particular Sadhana along with Kriyayoga. A farsighted genius as he was, Lahiri Baba did not want to disturb the normal tenor of life so long as it does not stand in the way of progress.

Shri Shri Lahiri Baba would normally ask his disciples to marry at the proper age and adopt the householder life, as, for most people, a virtuous married life leads gradually to non-attachment. He was, however, ready to make exception for those who had an overwhelming desire for adopting the life of a renunciate. Swami Pranavananda Giriji Maharaj was an instance in point.

The disciples of the Yogiraj who imbibed the real spirit of his teachings included his two sons, the Venerable Tinkori Lahiri and Dukori Lahiri Mahashays, Shrimat Swami Shri Yukteshwar Giriji Maharaj of Serampore, Shrimat Swami Pranavananda Giriji Maharaj, Shrimat Keshavananda Avadhut, Hangsa Swami

Kevalanandaji Maharaj (Shri Shri Shastri Mahashay), Acharya Shrimat Panchanan Bhattacharya Mahashay, Acharya Shrimat Bhupendranath Sanyal Mahashay, Shrimat Ramdayal Majumdar Mahashay (Dayal Maharaj), Shrimat Mahadev Prasadji and other highly advanced Yogis. Shrimat Bhupendranath Sanyal Mahashay attained his Mahasamadhi[1] a few years ago. His annotations on the *Gita*, following the Yogic interpretation of his Master, is an elevating Scripture to the spiritualists.

Judged from the point of view of the dissemination of Shri Shri Lahiri Mahashay's Sadhana and the ideals amongst the masses, Shrimat Swami Shri Yukteshwar Giriji Maharaj of Serampore, Bengal, was the mainspring and pillar of the Lahiri Empire. It was he who, with the help of his disciple Yogishwar Shrimat Shri Shri Matilal Thakur who was a constructive genius of the highest order, established the 'Satsanga Sabha' for the first time. He was called the 'Jnanavatar' due to his great researches in the spiritual field.

It was at the Kumbhamela[2] at Prayag (Allahabad) that Shri Yukteshwar met Babaji for the first time. Shri Yukteshwar did not as yet adopt the life of a Sannyasi, although his wife and only daughter were both dead. He heard somebody calling him as Swamiji instead of by his real name Priyanath. He was surprised and went to the Young Sadhu who was calling him. The Sadhu was none other than the great Babaji Maharaj himself. This fact was however known by Shri Yukteshwar much later when he met his Master Shri Shri Lahiri Mahashay. Shri Shri Babaji Maharaj conferred the title of Swamiji on Priyanath and asked him to write a book showing the underlying unity in the religions of the East and West. He promised to see him again when the book would be finished. He also sent a symbolic message through Shri Yukteshwar to his great disciple of the Yogiraj, of which we shall speak of later on. It was thus with the blessing of Shri Shri Babaji Maharaj that Shri Yukteshwar wrote the book *The Holy Science* or *Kaibalyadarshanam*. The day on which the book was finished, a strange incident happened. Shri Yukteshwar was going to take his bath in the Ganga,

---

1. Shrimat Bhupendranath Sanyal Mahashay entered Mahasamadhi on January 18, 1962.

2. A vast religious congregation of pilgrims and holy men every third year in India symbolising the flow of nectar of divine consciousness. Every twelfth year is a year for 'Purnakumbha' or 'full pitcher' of nectar.

Jnanavatar Shrimat Swami Shri Yukteshwar Giriji Maharaj

and lo! he found Babaji Maharaj himself standing beneath a tree. He at once laid himself prostrate before the Great Master and wanted to take him home. Shri Shri Babaji Maharaj would not agree. The shade of the tree, he said, was better for a Sannyasi like him. Shri Shri Yukteshwar Giriji Maharaj then appealed to him to kindly wait there for a few minutes. With great hurry he brought some sweets and fruits for Babaji Maharaj. But, alas, nobody could be seen there. Shri Yukteshwar asked many people nearby, but they did not see anybody with the likeness of Shri Shri Babaji. At this Shri Yukteshwar felt mortified. Later on, at the residence of Shri Shri Lahiri Mahashay at Benares, Shri Yukteshwar was sitting at the feet of his Master. Of a sudden, Babaji Maharaj appeared. At once Lahiri Baba rose and offered Pranams at his Lotus Feet. Shri Yukteshwar, however, did neither rise nor show any honor to the Great Babaji. The Yogiraj expressed his surprise at this seemingly strange behavior of Shri Yukteshwar. But Shri Shri Babaji Maharaj explained that Shri Yukteshwar was enraged against him as he could not find him at the treeshade at Serampore on coming back with sweets. This, however, as the great Babaji explained, was all the fault of Shri Yukteshwar himself. Babaji was there all the time. But Shri Yukteshwar had lost the concentration of his mind due to extreme hurry and that was the reason why he was unable to see the divine figure of Shri Shri Babaji Maharaj. Shri Yukteshwar felt ashamed at this and asked pardon from the Master of his Master.

Shrimat Swami Shri Yukteshwar Giriji Maharaj also brought about an edition of the *Shrimadbhagavadgita*, following the spiritual interpretation of his Master. Shri Shri Lahiri Mahashay himself revised the book and gave his blessings.

Shrimat Matilal Mukhopadhyaya was one of the first disciples of Shri Yukteshwar and had received the order of Shri Shri Lahiri Mahashay to be an Acharya when the great Yogiraj was no more in his human frame. Shri Yukteshwar was testing his disciple. There were many waiting to be initiated by Shrimat Matilal Thakur. But he did not as yet have any instructions from his Master to that effect. For many days the Master seemed to be so indifferent towards him. This seeming unkindness pained the disciple and he constantly prayed to Shri Shri Lahiri Mahashay so that his Gurudeva might again be kind to him. One night Shrimat Matilal was meditating in a closed room at Kidderpore where he was an

Yogishwar Shri Shri Matilal Thakur
Advent; Pous 15, 1273 B.S.
Mahasamadhi: Ashwin 23, 1352 B.S.

employee of the Kidderpore shipyard. Suddenly the divine figure of Shri Shri Lahiri Baba appeared amidst resplendent light, gave him his blessings, and initiated him as an Acharya. After this incident when Shrimat Matilal met his Gurudeva at his call, Shri Yukteshwar was highly pleased at this great change in his disciple and explained the Grace showered upon him by the Yogiraj. The Master knew it all. He was merely testing his disciple. Now he became very glad at his success and blessed him from the heart of his heart.

The life of Yogishwar Shrimat Matilal Thakur (Shri Shri Sachchidananda Deva) reveals before us an astounding spiritual personality fit to be a deep subject of study for any spiritual seeker. He was a householder with an ingrained spiritual tendency from his very birth. While serving at Burma he came in contact with the 'Fungi' Sadhus there. Later on he also became intimately connected with the religion of the Sikhs and the Theosophists. A great turning point came into his life when he lost his first child, a lovely son, within a year of his birth. Life lost its savor for him. The impermanence of life was so deeply impressed on his heart that he became the most earnest seeker of the life eternal, the life divine. At such a time he was initiated into Kriyayoga by Shrimat Swami Shri Yukteshwar Giriji Maharaj. He was then serving at Kidderpore. Very soon he so deeply applied himself to the organization of the 'Satsanga Sabha' under the instructions from his Master and made his colleagues and friends so inspired that he drew the appreciation of his Gurudeva as "Kidderpore is my right hand". Once while going to his office, he received in his heart a call from the Divine to work for the helpless and suffering humanity. The urge for responding to the call became so insistent that he was compelled to come back from the Serampore Railway Station carrying along a man attacked with blood-dysentery in his arms. The number of maimed and diseased people under his care gradually increased and at last he established the 'Bhaktashram', a charity home which he supported by begging alms from door to door. A time came when he had to leave his office and dedicate himself entirely to the service of the Divine. A few years passed, and then came another great change in the life of Shrimat Matilal Thakur. Shri Shri Lahiri Mahashay again appeared before him in his divine self and commanded him to establish 'Shrigurudham'. Accordingly, in Chantra, 1325 B.S.[1], "Shrigurudham (Yogada Satsanga)' was established at Serampore.

1. Shrigurudham was established in A.D. 1919

Yogiguru Shrimat Brahmachari Anilanandaji Maharaj

The Bhaktashram was now handed over to Shrimat Swami Abhedanandaji Maharaj, a great disciple of Shri Ramakrisna and the founder of the Shri Ramakrisna Vedanta Society. So long Shrimat Matilal has been ministering mainly to the physical disabilities of suffering humanity. Now he devoted himself entirely to the spiritual needs, which, when fulfilled, make for an all-round development of the human personality. Besides, the practice of Kriyayoga, even in its easier form as propagated by Shri Shri Lahiri Mahashay, is too much for the majority of ordinary mortals. They must be given a force in the human shape before which they can surrender and thus come gradually to the path of Sadhana. It is Shriguru who is that Force in its highest form. The establishment of Shrigurudham and its many branches all over West Bengal by Shri Shri Matilal Thakur has thus ushered in a new era in the evolution and propagation of Kriyayoga, and the tradition is being gloriously carried on by Yogiguru Shrimat Brahmachari Anilanandaji Maharaj, the greatest disciple of Yogishwar Shri Shri Matilal Thakur and the embodiment of Infinite Power and Infinite Grace. Shrimat Anilananda has established hundreds of centers for propagating the ideal of Shrigurudham and his magnetic spiritual personality has attracted millions to take shelter in his Grace. He has also established 'Shrigurumandir' (Shriguru Temple) at Shrigurudham premises at Serampore where images of the Yogiraj, Shri Yukteshwar and Shrimat Matilal Thakur have been installed in 1961. Brahmachari Anilanandaji knows no rest in fulfilling the task entrusted to him by his Master. He moves about everywhere, inspiring Faith and Love even in those who are averse to the Divine. One of the main centers established by him is the branch of Shrigurudham at 166, Belilios Road, Kadamtala, Howrah –1.

Yogishwar Shrimat Matilal Thakur has also been a great author of religious books including his *Atma-Katha* (Autobiography) which has been posthumously published by his disciple Shrimat Brahmachari Maharaj.

The name of Shrimat Paramhansa Yogananda Giriji Maharaj has spread through every corner of the world. It is through him that Shri Yukteshwar has made a gift of Shri Shri Lahiri Baba's message to the West – a duty which was entrusted to him by the Great Shri Shri Babaji Maharaj. Yoganandaji's father Sj. Bhagavati Charan Ghosh was a very high officer in the Railway. Once he refused to grant leave to one of his subordinates who wanted to go to his Gurudeva Shri Shri Lahiri Mahashay. Strangely enough, Bhagavati found the divine figure of the Yogiraj appear before him. "Bhagavati, you are very hard on your subordinates," said he. Henceforward Bhagavati turned to be a very devoted disciple to Shri Shri Lahiri Mahashay. Yoganandaji (Mukunda Lal Ghosh was his name before he adopted sannyasa) was laid at the feet of the Yogiraj when he was a mere child and the Master prophesied before the mother. "Your son will be an engine (for propagating the ideas of the Divine) in his later life." The prophecy came true. The divine engine in the frame of Shrimat Yoganandaji has been able to move even the hearts of those who were simply steeped in material civilization. And a great American product from his hand even now holds the sway of Self-Realization Fellowship[1] in the shape of President Daya Mata who graced the motherland of her Master for the first time by her loving and august visit in 1958.

Another great disciple of Shrimat Swami Shri Yukteshwar Giriji Maharaj is Shrimat Swami Satyananda Giriji Maharaj[2] who has still been ministering to the spiritual needs of millions and has given a concrete shape to Shri Yukteshwar's ideal of synthesis in his Ashram 'Sevayatan' at Jhargram, Midnapore (West Bengal). He is also an author of many books including the lives of Shri Shri Lahiri Mahashay and Shrimat Swami Shri Yukteshwar in Bengali.

Shrimat Panchanan Bhattacharya, the founder of Arya Mission, was one of the earliest disciples of Shri Shri Lahiri Mahashay. It was through him that most of the interpretations of Shri Shri Lahiri Baba on the Scriptures had been recorded and published. He himself was the author of many books including *Jagat O Ami* ("The world and I").

---

1. The reader is reminded here that the time of the first 1964 printing of this book in India, Self-Realization Fellowship, which was legally incorporated in the State of California on March 29, 1935, was the largest of several religious organizations in America that had emerged from the original Kriyayoga teachings of Paramhansa (Swami) Yogananda and Swami Dhirananda (Dr. Basu Kumar Bagchi). Now in 1997 with this First American Edition published by Amrita Foundation, Inc., there have emerged and are emerging many groups and organizations following the Kriyayoga teachings.

   – The Editor.

2. Shrimat Swami Satayananda Giriji Maharaj entered Mahasamadhi on August 2, 1971 – The Editor.

The teachings of Shri Shri Lahiri Mahashay found another able exponent in Shrimat Swami Pranavananda Giriji Maharaj whose great disciple Shrimat Jnanendranath Mukhopadhyaya, interpreter of the *Pranava-Gita*, is still in our midst, shedding spiritual luster over all around him.

But to come back to the Yogiraj himself. Although he shunned public gaze, the divine 'Leela' of Shri Shyama Charan spread far and near, without distinction of caste, creed or community. His superior officer in the office, too, was not deprived of his Grace. This Englishman had a soft corner for this efficient assistant who, even in the midst of multifarious duties in the office would always remain absent-minded, concentrated as he was in the Divine, thus earning for himself the title "Pagla Babu" (the eccentric Babu). Shri Shri Lahiri Baba once found his superior officer very depressed and asked him the cause of his depression. The officer told him that his wife had fallen very ill in England and he did not receive any news of her for a long time. The Yogiraj took pity on him and gave him the news of her recovery. He also quoted a few lines from her letter which was yet to be received by the officer. Later on, when the officer actually received the letter, he was surprised by discovering the language of "Pagla Babu" in the same. When, after some time, the lady came over to India, she could at once recognize the Yogiraj as the man whom she had seen at her bedside during illness and due to whose Grace she recovered. The officer was highly pleased to find such and exceptional Yogi in his own office.

After his own initiation at Ranikhet Shri Shri Lahiri Baba served the Government for some 25 years more. During his service life not many had the privilege of receiving initiation from him. It was only after his retirement, when he settled at Benares, that innumerable people came to take shelter under his divine Grace. Once or twice he had occasion to go to Krisnanagore and to Bisnupur in the district of Bankura in Bengal where his second son was married. He had also probably made a sojourn towards Munghyr and Bhagalpur. Even now, many Sadhakas are to be found in these places, especially at Bisnupur, who keep their Sadhana hidden from public gaze.

The Yogiraj once told a disciple about his own picture, "It will be your God if you believe, and a mere picture if you don't".

Some time later there was a sudden thunderfall near the house of that disciple. A daughter-in-law of the Yogiraj was present there at the time. She and a devoted woman of the house prayed earnestly before the picture of the Yogiraj for averting the danger. The thunderbolt fell on the same house, but the devotees were saved. They felt as if somebody had anointed them with cold ice which protected them from the deadly head of thunder.

A lady disciple of Shri Shri Lahiri Mahashay once prayed at his feet for him to save her future children. So far, unfortunately, she had no child alive. Lahiri Baba asked her to keep a strict watch over the lamp which burns in the room of the child's birth. In due time the lady gave birth to a child. A nurse, too, was engaged to look after the lamp which ought to have been kept burning all through the night. Towards the dawn, however, the tired mother and the nurse fell rather sleepy and the lamp was gradually going out. The door was closed from inside. Suddenly, however, the door banged open and the sleep of the women broke off. Surprised, they found the Gracious figure of the Yogiraj standing inside the room, silently pointing his finger towards the failing light of the lamp. At once they put the wick right and the lamp regained its luster. but where was the Yogiraj? There was no trace of him in the entire room. He only appeared for granting life to the child by making his devotee obey his command. The purpose was served and the child lived on. As a matter of fact, all his disciples considered him to be their only shelter in times of danger.

Shrimat Swami Shri Yukteshwar Giriji Maharaj once begged for the life of one of his friends. The Yogiraj at first asked him to get him treated by a doctor. But, the doctors gave no hope and Swamiji prayed insistently for his friend's life. At last his Gurudeva gave him just a small bottle of Neem Oil (Oil Margosa) and asked him to administer a few drops to his friend. On coming back from his Shrigurudeva Shri Yukteshwar found no sign of life in his friend. He grew indignant over his Master. Did he jest with him over the question of life and death of a man? However, he obeyed the Master's command and put a few drops of the oil through the lips of the dead. Great Heavens! what was the result? The friend gradually opened his eyes, and, few moments later, came to the Yogiraj in company with Shri Yukteshwar to render obeisance to his Lotus Feet. As the Yogiraj later explained to Shri Yukteshwar, the

Neem Oil was just an excuse for the satisfaction of Shri Yukteshwar. His divine Grace was the real medicine.

A lady devotee started for Benares for sitting at the Feet of her Master. While she was still on her way to the station, the train whistled. The lady prayed to her Shriguru with earnest devotion. Suddenly, the driver found that the train did not move an inch, although the wheels were revolving. After a thorough investigation which naturally took a long time, it was found that a screw had somehow got loose and that was the cause of all the trouble. However, during this hubbub, the lady had ample time to board the train. Just after she had finished her Pranam on reaching Benares, the Yogiraj smilingly advised her to be more punctual in her future journeys. What punctilious care for every detail in his disciples' lives and what a Grace to shower them with!

On the other hand there are many anecdotes to show how Shri Shri Lahiri Baba snapped the pride of people who had any form of vanity. Sj. Gangadhar Dey was a great painter and photographer of those times. The Yogiraj was generally averse to allowing his photograph to being taken. However, at the modest prayer of his disciples he agreed to pose before the camera. Before the snapshot was actually taken, he asked Gangadhar Babu about the method of photography. Gangadhar too explained the science of photography with great enthusiasm. A few moments later the snap was actually taken. But, to his utter surprise, Gangadhar Babu found that there was no reflection of the Yogiraj on the plate. He thoroughly examined his apparatus and experimented with other people, but no irregularity could be discovered. The Yogiraj was smiling a naughty smile. He asked the photographer, "what does your science tell you?" Gangadhar Babu was astounded. He understood that the power of material science is as nothing compared to the power of Yoga. Besides, the Yogiraj had attained an infinity which could not be circumscribed within the plate of a camera. However, Gangadhar Babu prostrated himself before this great Yogi and said, "Let science be damned. My pride has been shattered. Now be so kind as to allow your reflection to be caught in the camera."The Yogiraj agreed, and the photograph so familiar to us had its birth. The first prints were of a very small size, one of which may still be found in his house on the wall opposite his seat in the drawing room. Gangadhar Babu enlarged the first print later on in water-color which was preserved by Sj. Abhoy Charan Lahiri. He also prepared an oil-painting of the Yogiraj from this enlarged photograph.

Shri Shri Lahiri Mahashay had a disciple names Sj. Rammohan Dey whose younger brother Chandramohan passed brilliantly from the Lahore Medical College. Chandramohan, as instructed by his elder brother, came to offer Pranams to the Yogiraj and to receive his blessings. Lahiri Baba blessed him gladly from the heart of his heart. Chandramohan was narrating the recent developments in medical science and the extent to which he himself had imbibed them. Suddenly, the Yogiraj asked him about the signs which could distinguish the dead from the living. Chandramohan told him what he knew. Now the Yogiraj just stretched out his arm before the doctor and asked him to feel his pulse. Strangely enough, there was no beat in the pulse. Chandramohan brought forth a stethoscope and thoroughly examined his chest. But, no, there was no heart-beat as well. And yet, Shri Shri Thakur[1] was talking to him. After a good deal of meditation Chandramohan at last recalled a saying in his text-book that the signs of death enumerated there would not necessarily be applicable to the Yogis in India. The Yogiraj admonished him saying that Knowledge is limitless and therefore Chandramohan should always believe that he had learned only very little and the Vast Ocean of Knowledge was always lying before him. The instruction from the Yogiraj deeply influenced the young physician, and, by constant pursuit of knowledge, he later on became one of the foremost medical practitioners of his age in North-West India.

A great instance of the breaking of vanity is supplied by the episode of Kaviraj (a physician practicing the Ayurvedic[2] method of treatment) Pareshnath Roy who was a student of Gangadhar Sen, one of the greatest practitioners in Ayurveda. Kaviraj Pareshnath acquired great wealth and fame as a physician and scholar. But, added to his vast learning was also his great pride which made people quake in fear before him. Once it so happened that Sj. Rajchandra Sanyal, brother-in-law of Shri Shri Thakur, took him to this Pareshnath Kaviraj. The Kaviraj had written an annotation on Charaka, the great sage who wrote on medical science. He was reading out his annotation before a distinguished assembly of scholars and medical men all of whom praised it very highly. Finding the

1. Thakur means Avatar or Lord. – The Editor.

2. 'Ayurveda' is the indigenous medical science of India.

Yogiraj alone silent in the company, Pareshnath asked his impression about the book. Shri Shyama Charan gently replied, "It is entirely wrong". The people present there became afraid of the Kaviraj flaring up. Pareshnath was astounded for a moment. Nobody heretofore had the courage to utter such words before him. Angry and surprised, he asked the Yogiraj, "What do you know of this subject?" Again, the Yogiraj answered with a gentle smile, "O Yes, I know everything," and returned home.

A few days passed, days of great mental torture for the Kaviraj. Then he came to Shri Shyama Charan and submitted that his Professor Gangadhar Sen, after explaining Charaka, had actually told him that apart from his explanation, Charaka has some deeper significance which only a Yogi can explain. However, Pareshnath was eventually initiated by the Yogiraj and was counted among his most devoted disciples. The spiritual interpretation of Charaka as explained by Shri Shri Lahiri Mahashay was printed at some later date. Pareshnath gradually attained to the state of Samadhi and just because the Yogiraj had to go to his house, breaking his Samadhi and making him regain his normal state of consciousness, Pareshnath actually purchased a house near that of his Master and shifted there. Before his death Pareshnath bequeathed the major portion of his property to Sj. Tinkori Lahiri, the eldest son of the Yogiraj, by a will. Such incidents serve to show that the Yogiraj came to this world in order to indicate that all earthly possessions, riches or scholarship, become meaningless unless they are made subservient to a spirit of devotion, a spirit of humility before the Divine. Then and then alone they can yield their proper fruits. Besides, the Kaviraj, apart from his pride, was a really worthy man and the Yogiraj just showered his Grace upon him and changed the course of his life to the proper direction under the guise of breaking his vanity.

Once a man with a disreputable character came to the Yogiraj with a challenging attitude. As soon as he entered the room the Yogiraj asked his disciples to close their eyes. He would show them all a magic, he said. The newcomer too felt curious and closed his eyelids. Strangely enough, everybody present in the room had a similar experience. They all saw a lady clad in a colored sari and asked their Master the reason for it. The Yogiraj smilingly explained that the lady in question was the mistress of the newcomer who had an immoral relation with her. The pride of the man went to pieces at this unexpected display of Shri Shyama Charan's Yogic powers. He now felt repentant for his attitude of challenge, laid himself at the Feet of the Master and asked for initiation. The Yogiraj agreed to initiate him if he could extricate himself from the lady at least for six months at a stretch. If he would not be able to do that, there would be no need for initiation, said the Yogiraj enigmatically. The man observed the abstinence for a few months, but could not maintain it for the stipulated period of time. Very soon he fell seriously ill and succumbed to death. Thus, the words of the Yogiraj that it would not be necessary to initiate the man unless he would practice abstinence for six months, proved very true.

Sj. Abhoy Charan, the grandson of the Yogiraj, tells us of a great artisan disciple of Shri Shyama Charan named Subaran who joined the Franko-British Exhibition in England with his own woodcraft. The exhibition lasted for a long time, and Subaran came to India at regular intervals. After three such journeys to and back from England Subaran was once describing his experiences at the Fair and on the bosom of the Ocean. Incidentally, he said that in spite of so many journeys on the seas he had never had the experience of a typhoon which, according to the sailors, present an aspect of the terribly beautiful. Only a few days later after this description, Subaran had to start again for England. This time, however, a great typhoon arose in the Arabian Sea. The ship was about to be drowned. Everybody, including Subaran, was only thinking of saving his own life. The sailors asked the passengers to take the name of God. Subaran entered into a cabin nearby and with closed eyes prayed to the Gracious Lahiri Mahashay. Suddenly, he heard the voice of his Master and was surprised beyond measure to see him face to face on opening of his eyes. The Master asked him to come out of the cabin and watch the typhoon. Subaran felt ashamed of his desire and repeatedly prayed to excuse him. The Yogiraj rebuked him for being instrumental in endangering the lives of so many people. However, the storm had now almost subsided and Shri Shri Lahiri Mahashay asked Subaran to watch the sublime and the terrible aspects of God combined into a typhoon.

Sj. Abhoy Charan narrates an incident in which we come to know about Hitalal Sarkar, a golden-hearted disciple of the Yogiraj who served in a brick-making factory. He was all kindness to the poor and the distressed, and his excessive charity would sometimes be a cause of grief to his own family. He had only heard the name of the Yogiraj. Once at midday while supervising the work of the laborers, he felt a sudden and irresistible impulse for going somewhere he did not know. At once he had to start for the railway station. The booking clerk at the counter asked him about his destination. He, however, could not give the name of any place. Searching his pocket he found only Rupees eight and a few small coins. He wanted to have a ticket for any place which would be available within that amount. From the distracted appearance of Hitalal the middle-aged booking clerk had the impression that he was just searching out a place where he could pacify his lacerated mind. He, therefore, gave Hitalal a ticket for Benares, a place hallowed with the name of Lord Vishwanatha where Saints congregate from all corners of India.

The train for Benares started. Hitalal did not know where to go. He got down at Benares, took an Ekka[1] and directed it towards Bangalitola as that was the place which, as he had heard, was the main centre of the Bengalee residents at Benares. The Ekkaman led him up to the entrance of the lane leading to the house of the Yogiraj. Hitalal reached the end of the lane, walking, and was now thinking seriously where to go. That very moment the Yogiraj himself appeared at the entrance of his house and asked Hitalal to come in. The benign appearance of Shri Shyama Charan impressed the guest, and he asked the Yogiraj how he could know him. Shri Shri Thakur, however, asked him not to worry over such matters till he had finished his meals and taken rest. Every arrangement was made for his comfort. In the afternoon Hitalal found many learned gentlemen assembled before Shri Shri Lahiri Mahashay in his drawing room. He, however, understood nothing of the high-serious discussions conducted by the Yogiraj on spiritual matters. The next morning Hitalal accompanied Shri Shri Thakur for a bath in the Ganga. After this he was told by the Gracious Yogiraj that it was he who had brought Hitalal here by his spiritual force as the time was ripe for his initiation. Shri Hitalal Sarkar was thus initiated into Kriyayoga by a marvel of Divine Grace showered upon him. How inscrutable were the ways of the Incarnation of Yoga!

---

1. A horse-drawn carriage.

2. The play of Divine Grace.

The Leela[2] of Shri Shri Lahiri Mahashay is so endless and infinitely various that it would be impossible for any human being to give a detailed account of it. It is something to be pondered upon and meditated, to be felt along the blood. Many details, however, are still to be had from his devotees and spiritual descendants who are ever living united with the Infinite Consciousness and Grace that is Shri Shri Lahiri Mahashay. The Blessed Touch of such devotees would do more for a seeker than a perusal of his biographies. If, however, a biography of the Yogiraj creates a hankering in the reader's minds after getting into a personal contact with his great spiritual descendants, then and then alone its purpose would be amply fulfilled.

While in his mortal frame, the Yogiraj was the most highly respected citizen of Benares of his times. People would always accept his mediation in case of any religious dispute. Thus, we come to know of an assembly for religious discussions under his chairmanship where he convinced Shrimat Dayananda Saraswati, the founder of the 'Arya-Samaj', that his way of worshipping the Impersonal God was certainly not the only way for realizing the 'Sachchidananda'. The Divine who is everywhere can also be worshiped in different images according to the various tastes of the devotees. In this connection we come to know of an amusing incident which also gives us a taste of the miraculous Yogic powers of Shri Shri Lahiri Mahashay so sparingly used by him. Before starting discussions the Yogiraj had made a condition that only one should speak at a time in that assembly. In the heat of discussions, however, some of the followers of Shrimat Dayanandaji turned oblivious of that condition and spoke out conjointly to establish their point. The Yogiraj just asked them to stop speaking, and, strangely enough, they found themselves tongue-tied. After some time, the Yogiraj reminded them of the condition and gave them afresh the power of speech. Such tid-bits are scattered throughout the life divine of Shri Shri Lahiri Mahashay, and they may be taken as the "escapes of his inner power".

Thus for many years the Yogiraj was Gracious enough to scatter bliss amidst humanity and pave the way for a spiritual regeneration.

CHAPTER V

Mahasamadhi

In the preceding Chapter we referred to a symbolic message sent by Shri Shri Babaji Maharaj to his great disciple through Shri Yukteshwar at the Kumbhamela at Prayag. As soon as the message reached the Yogiraj, he suddenly assumed a very grave appearance and became absorbed in Samadhi. It seemed the message contained an indication of Shri Shri Lahiri Mahashay's disappearance from this mortal world. This reminds us of a similar symbolic message sent by Shri Shri Adwaitacharya to Shri Chaitanyadeva a few centuries back. Babaji Maharaj had a similar duty to perform. It was he who had brought the Yogiraj into this world for propagation of the mystery of Yoga. It was he again who commanded his beloved disciple to leave this earth when his mission was entrusted in able hands.

Many of the disciples of Shri Shri Lahiri Mahashay were in the know of his intention of leaving this mortal frame in the month of Ahswin, 1302 B.S. The Yogiraj had also told his wife about it six months before his Mahasamadhi and had asked her not to mourn for him; for, even after leaving this mortal frame, he would be always present shedding his benign Grace everywhere.

The immediate earthly cause of the Yogiraj's departure from this world, however, was a carbuncle on his back. He allowed himself to suffer for a month. When the disease took a serious turn, many of his disciples including his eldest son Sj. Tinkori Lahiri who was serving in the Postal Accounts Department in Calcutta at that time, and Shrimat Panchanan Bhattacharya were at his bedside at Benares. The famous Dr. Hemchandra Sen, M.D., also a disciple of the Yogiraj, came down from Calcutta for his treatment. As Shri Shri Lahiri Mahashay was unwilling to have an operation, the Neem-Oil prepared under his instructions was being applied to the wound. Dr. Purnachandra Banerjee, the family physician of Shri Shri Lahiri Mahashay, cleansed the wound and put a bandage over it. But as the Yogiraj felt uncomfortable at the bandage, he tore it off and made himself free.

While the Yogiraj was thus suffering, one of his famous physician disciples named Balgovinda who practiced Ayurveda earnestly appealed to him to stay on this earth at least as long as it took him to prepare a very rare medicine with high potency for him. He had already arranged for bringing one of the ingredients for the ointment from Ceylon. Shri Shri Lahiri Mahashay yielded to his fervent appeal, it seemed. The ingredient came and the ointment was prepared, but its application could not bring about the desired result.

Of those who nursed Shri Shri Lahiri Mahashay during his fatal illness, apart from his family members, the name of his Maharastrian disciple Krishnaramji has been especially mentioned by Sj. Abhoy Charan Lahiri. Even when the Yogiraj was in good health, Krishnaramji followed him as his shadow and Shri Shri Thakur, too, had great affection for this simple-minded Brahmin.

At last came the saddest day. It was the Mahastami, the second day of worship for the Divine Mother, Durga. The Puja was proceeding at the next house, the house of Sj. Rameshwar Chowdhury, the nearest neighbor of the Yogiraj. The most significant part of the Puja is conducted at the moment of transition from the 'Astami'[1] to the 'Navami'. It was just at this great auspicious juncture of "Sandhiksan" that the Yogiraj opened his eyes for the last time to look at this world in his human body and closed it finally, merging his consciousness in the Ocean of Eternity. The devotees looked on with an agonized feeling never again equalled in their lives.

For a long time the body retained its warmth and did not get stiff. The Yogiraj was taking a serene repose, it seemed. The disciples decorated him with garlands and sandalwood paste. People poured in from far and near to have a last look at the mortal remains of this God-man. The greatest living embodiment of Yoga in modern times was no more in his human frame.

A controversy started as to whether his body would be buried or cremated. Although cremation is the general rule for the common man in the Hindu community in India, the bodies of the great Saints

1. The eighth day of the dark or bright fortnight. Here it relates to the bright fortnight. So is Navami – the ninth day.

are generally given burials, as sometimes the Yogis perform many miraculous benefits to this world with the help of their bodies. But, although a Master of Yogis, Shri Shri Lahiri Mahashay was a householder, and therefore, many of his devotees advocated his cremation. His divine body was accordingly carried along with a grand procession to the Manikarnika Ghat and cremated there.

It is said that about six months before his Mahasamadhi the Yogiraj had once disclosed before his wife his intention of leaving this world within six months and instructed her so that his body might be given a burial within the compound of his own house. At the proper moment, however, everybody was so overwhelmed with grief that his instructions were forgotten.

After the body of the Yogiraj was cremated, Krishnaramji preserved some ashes and bones, mixed them up with sandalpaste and the soil of the Ganga, and rolled them into a ball decorating it with red sandalpaste. This remnant of the holy body is still with his descendants. Many other disciples of the Yogiraj preserved portions of the holy ashes and bones.

It was on the 26th of September 1895 (1302 B.S.). The Yogiraj was no more in his human frame. But just at the moment of his departure his divine figure was seen by three of his disciples at different places. Shrimat Swami Pranavananada Giriji Maharaj had just received the news of his Guruji's illness and was preparing to leave for Benares. The astral figure of the Yogiraj appeared before him and said, "There's no hast; I have left my mortal frame". He consoled the devotee by telling him that he is always present, in spite of the absence of his human body. Shrimat Panchanan Bhattacharya and Shrimat Keshavananda Avadhut were also blessed with similar visions.

That is also the consolation for many who did not have the great good fortune of having his personal contact. For even now, apart from radiating his influence through his spiritual descendants and through a general Grace showered upon the world, the Yogiraj shows his Leela in a thousand and one forms before people whose minds are devoted to the path of Truth. Sj. Abhoy Charan has mentioned a few specially important incidents in this book which may briefly be recalled here.

A life-size oil painting of the Yogiraj is kept in the drawing room of his house. Every year women devotees of the household observe fasting on the Mahastami Day, and, after worshipping the Yogiraj during the Sandhiksan, break their fast. It so happened one year that the Sandhiksan fell exactly at the time when the Yogiraj actually passed away from the human world (at 4-20-24 seconds in the afternoon). The ladies were highly surprised to find that just at the Sandhiksan the oil-painting of Shri Shri Lahiri Mahashay gradually disappeared in a thick mask of clouds. Some two minutes later, however, as the Sandhiksan passed away, the cloudy covering wore off fully revealing the picture of Shri Shri Lahiri Mahashay again.

Once at the time of opening a new window in the wall of the drawing room the portrait of Shri Shri Lahiri Mahashay was removed from its former position so that it might be more clearly visible in the light coming through the window. But, strangely enough, on that very date and the next day, too, all the members of the Lahiri family, wherever they were, started receiving slight injuries. The implications were realized, and the portrait was restored to its former place.

Shrimati Kashimoni Devi, the holy consort of the Yogiraj, attained her Mahasamadhi at the ripe old age of ninety-four. For a few years before this, she was generally attended to by somebody in the house. Only for some two hours at noon nobody would be there by her side. One day before noon she asked her grandson Sj. Abhoy Charan to place the best woolen 'Asan' (seat) by her bedside and leave the room. Both Abhoy Charan and his wife asked grandma the reason for this. Who could be coming to pay homage to her at that odd hour of the day? But they were startled to hear that every noon, when the room would be deserted by visitors and attendants, the holy figure of Shri Shri Lahiri Mahashay would creep in through the northern casement and spend some time in conversation. He, however, disappeared whenever there was a possibility of a visitor coming in. Since that day the woolen seat was kept separate for the Yogiraj and nobody else was allowed to take his seat on it.

Shri Utpal Sanyal, son of the youngest daughter of Sj. Abhoy Charan Lahiri Mahashay had, in his childhood days, mystic communion with the Yogiraj. When he was a mere three-year-old child, he would often enter a solitary chamber of their house and hold conversations with the great Shri Shri Lahiri Mahashay whom he described as "Shyam Baba". One evening Utpal's parents were going to a cinema show. Utpal, however, entered his room for Shyam Baba's permission and after a time told his parents that Shri Shyama Charan wanted him not to go to the cinema. The boy did not go. He remained at home with his grandmother. At the end of the show, however, his parents came home, thoroughly drenched with a sudden heavy shower of rain.

Utpal came to Benares when he was about five years old. As soon as he noticed the statue of the Yogiraj, he recognized him as his "Shyam Baba". With the advance in years, however, Utpal did not have the good fortune of holding such communions with Shri Shri Lahiri Mahashay. This perhaps shows that, as the poet says, "Heaven lies about us in our infancy", but "shades of the prison-house begin to close upon the growing boy", when it becomes necessary for him to revive his divine consciousness with 'Sadhana'.

Of course, any Sadhana again depends ultimately on His Grace. The words "गुरुकृपा हि केवलम्" are true, very true. Nothing can be done without the Grace of the Master. And the Master is ever ready to shower his Grace upon us if only we are simple and sincere at heart.

The incidents related above show us beyond a doubt that the Yogiraj has only left his mortal frame, but he is there in Cosmic Consciousness, ready to bless us with divine inspiration. We are now at the juncture of a new era. The human consciousness is suffering the trammels of a new birth. On one side there is corruption boiling and bubbling, "अभ्युत्थानमधर्मस्य" (the rise of corruption), as Lord Krisna said in the *Gita*, but on the other, the divine magnetism has been doing this work through man-making, moulding the characters of men in order to make them fit for receiving the divine Power and Grace. The Yogis believe that we are in the early years of the ascending 'Dwapara'[1] when the human consciousness will gradually have a lift. Yogiraj Shri Shri Lahiri Mahashay had his advent at

1. We shall discuss the different stages of human consciousness in different ages in the Appendix.

a period of transition from darkness into light and it is his Grace which continues to shine upon us, poor mortals, as a beacon-light on the path of Truth.

May we feel his benign presence in our midst, illuminating every moment of our lives with the Bliss that is He. Amen.

APPENDIX

In the preceding Chapter we have spoken about the Age 'Dwapara' when the human consciousness is gradually on the ascent. Let us take up a brief discussion of the ages in relation to human consciousness as enunciated by the Great Yogis.

It was Shrimat Swami Shri Yukteshwar Giriji Maharaj, the great disciple of the Yogiraj, who first explained the facts about the Yugas or the Cycles of human consciousness on earth in modern times. He noticed the miscalculations regarding the Yugas in our current almanacs and sought to rectify them in the light of Truth. He also published some rectified almanacs and prophesied that a day would come when this perfectly scientific system based on astronomical observations would be current throughout the world. We have a detailed enunciation of his theory in the introduction to his book *The Holy Science* or *Kaibalyadarshanam*. The same theory has been very beautifully expounded by his disciple Shrimat Matilal Thakur in his *Yuga-Paribartan O Jagadgurur Abirbhav* (The Evolution of the Ages and the Holy Advent of the Master of the Universe). Shrimat Paramhansa Yoganandaji, too, has mentioned about the theory in his *Autobiography of a Yogi.*

The following is only a brief sketch of what the Master has said. An inquisitive reader may kindly look into the books mentioned above for further details.

Oriental astronomy tells us that the Sun, with all its planets and their moons, takes some star for its dual and revolves round it in about 24,000 earthly years. Another motion of the Sun makes it revolve round a Grand Centre called 'Visnunabhi' or the seat of the Creative Power Brahma, the Universal magnetism. When the Sun in its revolution round its dual comes nearest to this centre (which takes place when the autumnal equinox comes to the first point of Aries), 'dharma' becomes so developed that man can easily comprehend the mysteries of the Spirit. After 12,000 years the Sun goes farthest from the Grand Centre and therefore man cannot grasp anything besides gross material creation. Again the Sun advances towards the Grand Centre and human consciousness, too, gradually advances till it is complete in another 12,000 years.

Each of these periods of 12,000 years is called one of the Daiva Yugas or Electric Couple and brings about a complete change in the human world. Thus we have one electric cycle of 12,000 years in an ascending arc, and 12,000 years in a descending arc.

The gradual development of 'dharma' is divided into four different stages in a period of 12,000 years. The time of 1,200 years during which the Sun passes through the 1/20th portion of its orbit is called the 'Kali Yuga' when 'dharma' is at its lowest (स्थूल). The next 2,400 years (2/20th portion) is called 'Dwapara' when the human conciousness can comprehend fine matters or electricities and their attributes (सूक्ष्म). The next 3,600 years (3/20th portion of 24,000 years) is the 'Treta Yuga' when the human intellect can comprehend the divine magnetism, the source of all electrical forces (कारण). The period of 4,800 years is called the 'Satya Yuga' when 'dharma' is at its highest (तुरीय) and the human consciousness can comprehend God the Spirit in His full glory. The state of consciousness referred to in the above lines, however, concern only the common run of human consciousness. Great Yogis or spiritualists may flourish in every age and they are always exceptions. They are never bound down by Space and Time and therefore can transcend the general virtues of the particular periods to which they belong.

The theory of the Yugas has been beautifully explained by the great sage Manu in his *Manusamhita*:–

> "चत्वार्याहुः सहस्राणि वर्षाणान्तु कृतं युगम् ।
> तस्य तावच्छती सन्ध्या सन्ध्यांशश्च तथाविधः ॥
> इतरेषु ससन्ध्येषु ससन्ध्यांशेषु च त्रिषु ।
> एकापायेन वर्तन्ते सहस्राणि शतानि च ॥" (1.69-70)

The Satya-Yuga consists of 4,000 years. But 400 years before and after the Yuga are its 'Sandhis' or periods of mutation with the preceding and the succeeding Yugas. Thus the Satya-Yuga continues for 4,800 years. In calculating the other Yugas and Yuga-Sandhis, the numerical 'I' should be deducted from the numbers of both thousands and hundreds indicating the periods of the previous Yugas and Sandhis. According to this calculation the duration of the Treta comes to 3,000+300+300=3,600 of the Dwapara 2,000+200+200=2,400 and that of the Kali becomes 1,000+100+100=1,200 years.

The current almanacs give us the Kali Yuga itself as consisting of 432,000 years instead of only 1,200 years. The error, too, was due to the influence of Kali or the dark age when the human intellect lost the power to grasp finer things. Thus, Medhatithi and Kullukabhatta, two of the celebrated commentators on the *Manusamhita* were both wrong in taking the earthly years mentioned in the verses as "Daiva" or years of the gods which have never been mentioned in the Samhita in this context. The *Mahabharata*, in the Vanaparva (Chapter 188) and Shantiparva (Chapter 231, Verses 20-23), and the *Harivamsha* tell us the same thing as the great sage Manu does. From a detailed discussion of all these sources the Masters have shown us that the cycles of human consciousness on earth move on in the following order: Satya, Treta, Dwapara, Kali (the descending arc); Kali, Dwapara, Treta, Satya (the ascending arc). Thus we find that we have two Kalis and two Satyas side by side, the one ascending, the other a descending one. We have just now finished 2,400 years of Kali (1,200 descending and 1,200 ascending) and in 1969 are passing through the 269th year of the Dwapara Era. Signs of gradual improvement in the general human consciousness were visible in the 1,200 years of the ascending Kali. As soon as 1,100 years of the ascending Kali were spent, the period of mutation preparing for the Dwapara Age started and finer electrical matters gradually received greater and greater comprehension from the human mind.

It was about the year 1600 A.D. that Williams Gilbert discovered magnetic forces and observed the presence of electricity in all material objects. Kepler's astronomical laws came about in 1609. We had also the telescope of Galileo. Drebbel of Holland gave us the microscope in 1621. Newton's Law of Gravitation came in 1670. The steam was used by Thomas Savery in raising water about 1700. In 1720, Stephen Gray discovered the action of electricity on the human body. The political and the cultural life of man, too, started showing marked developments till we have reached the present stage when the idea of one-world is no more a ridiculous theme. True it is that the world is constantly being rent asunder by ghastly and brutal wars. True that the atoms and the space race amongst different nations threatens humanity with a complete annihilation. But these disturbances are inevitable when out of large-scale disasters a new era will spring up over the ruins of the old. We have just now passed the 200 years of transition at the beginning of the age and have just entered the 64th year of the real Dwapara. Corruption flourishes everywhere. Death and devastation, dishonesty and brutality have become the order of the day. They will perhaps increase and come to a head. But on the other hand the world is ripe for a new advent. In about 25 years, as Yogishwar Shri Shri Matilal Thakur Maharaj has said, we are going to have a full manifestation of the Divine in the human from the supreme power over this Universe. And peace will prevail in the end. This is according to the promise made by Lord Krisna to Arjuna in the *Gita*. Whenever the world will be in the grip of men thoroughly unprincipled and anti-divine, whenever the rise of corruption will reach its climax and the honest men will groan under tyranny, the Divine will manifest Himself in His full force amidst the human beings and save the world from utter destruction.

"यदा यदा हि धर्मस्य ग्लानिर्भवति भारत।
अभ्युत्थानमधर्मस्य तदात्मानं सृजाम्यहम्॥
परित्राणाय साधुनां विनाशाय च दुष्कृतां।
धर्मसंस्थापनार्थाय सम्भवामि युगे युगे॥"

The same promise has also been made by the Mother Force of the Divine in the *Chandi* (a portion of the *Markandeya Purana*):

"इत्थं यदा यदा वाधा दानवोत्था भविष्यति।
तदा तदावतीर्याहं करिष्याम्यरिसंक्षयम्॥"

Whenever the devilish forces are let loose, the Mother Force of the Divine will have a supreme manifestation for the protection of the just and the righteous.

But before that supreme manifestation is possible, the Divine comes in our midst in the shape of great sages and prepares the seeds for receiving the Bliss Divine. It was therefore at a period of great transition that Yogiraj Shri Shri Shyama Charan Lahiri Mahashay was born. Other sages, too, are doing the same work. They are preparing some souls at least in which the Divine can fix His throne. There was Shri Ramakrisna who by his own life showed the modern world the fundamental unity in all religions. After all, 'Dharma' is one and indivisible. We are all children of the same Creator. The differences touch only the skin, the core remains intact. The differences are due to the differences in customs and manners, in circumstances which must vary from age to age from country to country. The Creator has not created a machine. The Universe is living in Him the Great 'Dharma' (the force that upholds the entire Universe), who is at once One (एकमेवाद्वितीयम्) and 'many' ("बहु स्याम्, प्रजायेय"), and therefore variety is its birthright. But the Indian message of the fundamental unity in variety in the field of 'Dharma' has first been shown to the world by Swami Vivekananda, the greatest disciple of Shri Ramakrisna, from the Vedanta, the repository of the knowledge of Atman. The advent of the Yogiraj has a deeper significance for us as he came to teach the particular stage of Sadhana for the Age of Dwapara. The Shastras tell us that it is Rajayoga which is to be the most suitable and predominant form of Sadhana for this age. Lord Krisna instructed Arjuna in Rajayoga in the last Dwapara. Before that for many years this was forgotten among the masses. Shri Krisna revived it for human welfare:

"स कालेनेह महता योगो नष्टः परन्तप ॥
स एवायं मया तेऽद्य योगः प्रोक्तः पुरातनः ।
भक्तोऽसि मे सखा चेति रहस्यं ह्येतदुत्तमम् ॥" (The *Gita*: IV,2,3)

Just because Yoga is the most suitable Sadhana for the development of human consciousness in Dwapara it has been revived by the Yogiraj. In this respect it is he who occupies the most important position in our age. Swami Vivekananda paved the way before the West by the Vedanta. Paramhansa Yogananda sowed the seeds of Yoga in the field. And it is the message of the Yogiraj that is even now propelling human consciousness in and outside India to a great Self-Consciousness. And with what a love for the common man! Somebody came and accused the Yogiraj of giving Kriyayoga to some unworthy man. "Well", said the Incarnation of Grace, "had I not given him that, he would have been worse."

Another fact must be mentioned before the book comes to a close. The *Gita* has now been a catchword throughout the world. It has been translated into all the major languages of the world, read and appreciated and commented upon by all great thinkers. But the sole credit of taking it out of the groove of scholars and placing it before the public for the first time goes to the Yogiraj himself. It was not merely that he gave his spiritual interpretation to the *Gita*, published by many of his disciples. He himself printed a few thousand copies of the *Gita* (only the original) in Bengali and Hindi scripts and distributed them freely amongst the public. A very significant act for the Yogavatar of the Dwapara Era.

The ideals of the Yogiraj, showing us as they do the path of eternal light and truth, will continue to influence the ages yet unborn, and countries yet unexplored. His Cosmic Consciousness is blessing us, one and all, with the gift of Faith, the one thing needed in this chaotic world at present.

We are not afraid. We are at the Feet of the Living Message of the Yogiraj in the person of our Master Yogiguru Anilananda. Let His Name be glorified. "Joy Guru" (Victory to my master).

BOOKS INTERPRETED BY SHRI SHRI LAHIRI MAHASHAY

1. Shrimadbhagavadgita.

2. Pataniala Yogasutra:
Published by Shrimat Panchanan Bhattacharya:
1291 B.S., Shaka 1806.

3. Vaishesika Darshana:
Published by Shrimat Panchanan Bhattacharya;
1295 B.S. Expenses borne by a rich devotee in Calcutta.

4. Manusamhita or Manu Rahasya:
1295 B.S., No name of the publisher in the printed books.
In the Manuscript Sj. Lalitmohan Bandyopadhyaya has been mentioned as the writer and Sj. Prasaddas Goswami as the reviser.

5. Paniniya Shiksa:
Published by Shrimat Panchanan Bhattacharya: 1295 B.S.

6. Markandeya Chandi:
Published by Shrimat Panchanan Bhattacharya: 1297 B.S.

7. Upanisads:
Krisna-Yajurvediya Tejovindu, Dhyanavindu and Amritavindu Upanisads:
Published by Shrimat Panchanan Bhattacharya: 1997 B.S.

8.Kabir:
The Hindi original in the Bengali script with ordinary and Yogic meaning in Bengali (Part 1) – Published by Shrimat Panchanan Bhattacharya: 1297 B.S.

9. Taittiriya Upanisad:
The original with Yogic interpretation – Published by Shrimat Panchanan Bhattacharya: 1299 B.S.

10. Vedantadarshana:
Original with interpretation – Published by Sj. Mahendranath Sanyal, Serampore : 1299 B.S.

11. Omkar-Gita:
Published by Shrimat Panchanan Bhattacharya: 1300 B.S.

12. Guru-Gita:
Published by Shrimat Panchanan Bhattacharya: 1300 B.S.: 1893 A.D.

13. Astabakra-Samhita:
Published by Shrimat Panchanan Bhattacharya: 1300 B.S.: 1893 A.D.

14. Abinashi Kabir-Gita:
Published by Shrimat Panchanan Bhattacharya: 1300 B.S.
Expenses borne by Sj. Kumudnath Maitra, Zamindar, Patul, Rajsahi.

15 Abadhut-Gita:
Printed at the expenses of Talukdar Chitrasen Sinha, an inhabitant of Dharna in the district of Faijabad.

16. Tantrasar (including **Yantrasar** within itself):
Published by Shrimat Panchanan Bhattacharya.

17. Mimamsartha-Samgraha (**Niralambopanisad** within the same) Published probably by Shrimat Panchanan Bhattacharya.

18. Lingapurana:
Published by Shrimat Panchanan Bhattacharya.

19. Japaji (The first book by Guru Nanak):
Sj Chitrasen Sinha paid Rs. 100/- for printing the book.

20. Gautamasutra:
Published by Shrimat Panchanan Bhattacharya. Printed at the expenses of Sj. Annadaprasad Sen, Zamindar of Rangpur.

21. Charaka:
Published by Shrimat Panchanan Bhattacharya: 1297 B.S.

22. Sankhyadarshana:
Published by Shrimat Panchanan Bhattacharya: 1295 B.S.
Sj. Dayalchand Das of Chinsura paid Rs. 100/- for printing this book.

BIBLIOGRAPHY

1. **Atma Katha:**
Yogishwar Shri Shri Matilal Thakur.

2. **Autobiography of a Yogi:**
Paramhansa Yogananda

3. **Shri Shri Shyama Charan Lahiri Mahashay:**
Shrimat Swami Satyananada Giri

4. **Shri Shri Shyama Charan Lahiri:**
Shrimat Anandamohan Lahiri, (1927:73/2, Beniatola Street, Calcutta)

5. **The Life-History of the Revered Yogiraj Shri Shri Shyama Charan Lahiri Mahashay:**
Sj. Abhoy Charan Lahiri (D 31/58 Madanpura, Benares, Basanta-Panchami, 1364 B.S.)

6. **Introduction to the "Pranava-Gita" by Shrimat Swami Pranavananda Giri Paramhansa:**
Shrimat Jnanendranah Mukhopadhyaya
(50 Raja Basanta Roy Road, Calcutta)

7. **Anjali:**
1338 B.S.: Published by Gurudham, Puri: Prayer by Prof. Narayan Das Bandyopadhyaya included in the book.

EDITIONS PUBLISHED BY AMRITA FOUNDATION, INC.

The original, unchanged writings of
Paramhansa (Swami) Yogananda

The Second Coming of Christ, Vol.1
The Second Coming of Christ, Vol.2
The Second Coming of Christ, Vol.3

The Sermon on the Mount (Interpretations of)

Metaphysical Meditations (1932 First Edition)
Divine Perceptions – Interpretations of Genesis, Revelation and the Bhagavad-Gita
PRAECEPTA® Lessons of Paramhansa Yogananda

The original, unchanged writings of Swami Yogananda Giri
and Swami Dhirananda Giri, Associate (Dr. Basu Kumar Bagchi)

The Science of Religion (1920 First Edition)
Psychological Chart (1921 First Edition)
Songs of the Soul (1923 First Edition)
Scientific Healing Affirmations (1924 First Edition)
Whispers From Eternity (1929 First Edition)
PRAECEPTA® BOOK (1923 First Edition)

The original, unchanged writings of Swami Dhirananda
(Dr. Basu Kumar Bagchi)

Philosophic Insights (1925 First Edition)
Glimpses of Light (1929 First Edition)
Raja Yoga Series (1929 First Edition)

The Hound of Heaven by Francis Thompson
(An early 1900's English edition)

Yogiraj Shri Shri Lahiri Mahashay by J.C. Bhattacharya
(1964 First Edition)

Kabīr: In the Light of Kriyayoga by J.C. Bhattacharya
(1974 First Edition)